Towards
a new
revolution

FORTRESS

Towards a new revolution

Elizabeth
Clarke
&
Richard
Peters

FORTRESS

Towards a new revolution
Workers of the Soviet Union speak

Elizabeth Clarke & Richard Peters

First published April 1990

Text, translations and photographs © Fortress Books

ISBN 1-870958-09-8

Published and distributed by Fortress Books
PO Box 141 London E2 0RL (01 985 7394)

Printed in Great Britain by Biddles Ltd
of Guildford and Kings Lynn

Cover design by Michael Moore
Cover photograph © AP Wirephoto

Fortress Books is a socialist publishing house. We encourage readers of our works to actively participate in the struggle for socialism. If you would like to receive more information about the ideas and events in this book, or have any comments and suggestions, you are welcome to contact the authors via Fortress Books, PO Box 141, London E2 0RL.

Contents

Introduction 1

First impressions 6

The workers' leaders meet 14

The 'Democratic Union' 25

With the students 29

Searching for a programme 34

Organising in the factories 46

The middle layers 53

At the Scientific Institute 57

In Moscow 70

Moscow life 79

The movement on the streets 86

State repression 95

To the Donbas coalfield 100

The miners' battles 110

Return to Leningrad 118

Postscript 124

Appendix One: Terry Fields' letter 127

Appendix Two: The Trade Union *Justice* 129

Appendix Three: The Trade Union *Independence* 132

Appendix Four: The Donbas strike committee 134

Bibliography 137

Introduction

REVOLUTION HAS BURST on the Stalinist world like a thunderstorm that rolls and roars across the heavens. Mighty movements have breached the granite walls built over decades to protect tyrants and parasites from public challenge. The fate of rulers has been decided on the streets.

Programmes, ideas, parties, leaders – old and new – are being subjected to the scrutiny of a population for generations under the iron heel of Stalinist reaction.

If this applies in all the countries of Eastern Europe – without exception now – what of the USSR – the homeland of the socialist revolution, and the birthplace, too, of Stalinism and all the horrors that that has entailed for more than sixty years? How will the drama unfold there now that the curtain is being blown open by events?

Perestroika and *Glasnost* have provided a mountain of information, statistics and revelations. From the television and newspapers, we can discern some of the processes at work and build up an outline picture of the situation. But there is no substitute for a first-hand assessment. Only then is it possible to fill in the detail, add the colour and, where necessary, even adjust the outline itself.

This book is the product of a visit to the Soviet Union towards the end of 1989 by two members of the British labour movement. We are Marxists and base ourselves on a Trotskyist analysis of the nature of the USSR – its historical origins and the situation that exists today.

We travelled therefore, not like ordinary visitors – to visit the art galleries, theatres, concert halls and cathedrals, and wonder at the architectural grandeur of Leningrad and Moscow – much as we admired them in passing! Our intention was to return to Britain with a much clearer idea and a deeper understanding of how the explosive movement developing in the Soviet Union will unfold through discussions with some of its most active participants.

But why write even a small book about it when so much else has been written already? The struggles of the working class of any

1

country – especially a proletariat at least 120 million strong – are of interest to workers of all countries. These struggles and the moods and the aspirations of the workers involved are the least reported by the commentators of the East or the West. Rulers throughout the world maintain a conspiracy of silence, sharing a mortal fear of the power of the working class and of the 'infection' of revolutionary ideas.

The working people of Britain are moving into new battles. The outcome of their struggles could be massively influenced by the success or failure of the political revolution in the Soviet Union. There is a keen interest to know much more than what is being conveyed at the present time. It is our purpose to throw as much light as possible on the underlying processes at work for the benefit of as wide an audience as possible. We have in mind particularly those workers already searching for an answer to the fundamental questions that present themselves today.

No one, least of all the authors of this book, would pretend that a short visit to the USSR can provide all the answers. We do not claim that our account is neutral. We have tried to 'tell it as it is', and to hide nothing. But we set out with a very distinct standpoint, a specific analysis and set of ideas, to be tested against reality.

We see the successful socialist revolution of October 1917 as the greatest event in human history. The elimination of landlordism and capitalism and the establishment of the state-owned planned economy was an historic conquest. It brought the USSR in huge strides from the level of an India to the second largest super-power in the world. Thus, it literally changed the course of history, so much followed in other parts of the world as a direct product of the establishment of state ownership and a plan.

The origins of Stalinism

The subsequent isolation of the revolution to the realms of a previously backward economy, however, placed intolerable burdens on the emerging workers' state. War and deprivation drained the energies of the heroic proletariat, who had originally exercised real workers' power through the soviets. The 'classical' development of the socialist revolution would have been possible only on the basis of big material improvements. Without the spread of the revolution to any one of the advanced capitalist countries, shortages prevailed, and a caste of military men and bureaucrats arose to police society.

Stalin and his entourage elbowed aside the genuine representatives of Bolshevism and of the working class. Through his ruthless, brutal measures – above all the purges and the forced collectivisation of agriculture – power was concentrated in his hands and millions perished.

Managed in a bureaucratic manner, the economy nevertheless had expanded during the five-year plans at a rate unknown in the capitalist world. This was at two or three times the cost of capitalism.

All the principles of democratic socialism that Lenin and Trotsky had fought for had been crushed. Lenin's widow Krupskaya commented that even Lenin would have been in one of Stalin's labour camps, had he not died in 1924! Trotsky and his co-thinkers in the Left Opposition had been reviled and exterminated. Trotsky himself was assassinated 50 years ago this year. Exiled and driven from country to country, he had devoted his life to an unrelenting combat against Stalinism.

This analysis was our starting point. The planned economy has displayed enormous advantages over the chaos and anarchy of capitalism. Private ownership was and still is incapable of developing the economy of the USSR. We as socialists stand firmly by these beliefs and adamantly defend public ownership and planning as the necessary prerequisites for socialism. But what exists in the Soviet Union is not socialism; it is a monstrous perversion of socialism. Stalin and all the heads of state that followed him have presided over a society in which the working class has been excluded from power, and in which the gap between the pampered and privileged ruling layer and the ordinary working people is as great, if not greater, than in the capitalist countries themselves.

By basing themselves on the state owned planned economy, the bureaucracy have, in the past, succeeded in developing the economy and taking society forward. It had been only a 'relative fetter'. We understood, before we made our visit, that the bureaucracy had now become a major road-block, an absolute fetter on the further development of the economy and of society. Only through its removal by the mighty working class of the USSR, in the course of the political revolution, could socialism become a reality in the land of October.

Gorbachev's accession to power in 1985 marked a qualitative new phase in the development of society in the Soviet Union. It did not signify, as some believed, the coming to power of a genuine representative of working people, who would somehow lift the bureaucracy from their backs without breaking the resistance of the workers. The Gorbachev reforms were introduced on behalf of the bureaucracy of which he was an astute representative, in order to maintain the rule of the bureaucracy. Without them, and with the economy moving into crisis, revolution from below threatened the future existence of this privileged elite.

Gorbachev's 'opening up', *Glasnost*, was an attempt to reorganise the economy – leaning on the support of the masses to deal a blow at the old corrupt layer that stood in the way. These measures have unleashed forces which Gorbachev could well be incapable of reining in at a later stage.

These were the views with which we set out on our journey. Marxism is not a fossilised set of theories, but a guide to action. It provides the instruments with which to analyse living processes. It has nothing in common with the stultifying, static approach of the reformist or the bureaucrat, who can think only in fixed categories. True Marxism embraces reality with all its complications. Sticking stubbornly to pre-conceived ideas, or abandoning principles in order to adapt to the mood of the moment, are equally disastrous courses for anyone claiming to be a Marxist.

The situation we met provided us with many insights. Much of what we thought was confirmed. But much was also shattered and swept away! Our ideas were corrected, filled out and enriched. Because of our particular political point of view, and because we discussed with people as committed fighters in the struggle for workers' democracy and socialism, we evinced responses and observed details that visitors from other standpoints may not have done.

Lies, distortions, humbug and hypocrisy have screened the truth for so long from the long-suffering masses of the Soviet Union. The veil is being lifted by the force of the workers' movement itself. We hope we have been able to shed a particular light on the events that will unfold. No Marxist would wish to predict the exact course that history is going to take. But the material presented here, combined with a Marxist analysis, gives a better idea of what is going on now in the USSR and, above all, of what is likely to be the possible course of events. Undoubtedly the future will be stormy, as a period of revolution and counter-revolution has opened up.

We were there towards the end of 1989 – a momentous year of dramatic election results and the great miners' strike that shook the ruling bureaucracy to the core. The highlights of our visit were undoubtedly our conversations with workers' leaders in the independent trade unions and the miners' strike committees.

Our account attempts to show how, each day, new facets of life and politics were revealed to us. It is not, however, a chronological diary. We have noted some of our opinions and conclusions when it has seemed appropriate.

We include in our narrative examples of one or two of the

obstacles we encountered and also some observations on everyday life, for which we make no apology. We also include a few references to history as we met it on our way. It is human beings, after all, that make history and history that makes human beings. It is up to the reader to judge the merits of the end result.

Acknowledgements

We are extremely grateful to all those who made our visit possible and effective. There are those who contributed time and effort in preparing us to do the work. Of necessity travelling without political books or material with us, we needed to register many points thoroughly in our minds.

There are those who painstakingly went over the manuscript in order to rescue the essential from the inessential. To them, particularly Lynn Walsh and Peter Taaffe, we are gratefully indebted.

We wish to thank all those who made things easier for us, who looked after our practical as well as our political needs during our visit. We must also thank those who made things more difficult, too – who put us to the test – challenging all our preconceptions and demanding clear answers to their own questions. They forced us to question our own views and to clarify them. Unfortunately, we cannot always identify them by their full or actual names. Many of the people we spoke to are fearless militants, but we would not want to add to the difficulties they have to contend with already. After our return, a prominent leader of Leningrad's independent unions was beaten up in circumstances which his friends described as decidedly 'suspicious'. Walking alone, he was knocked out with a blow to his head and his nose was broken. He had to spend three days in hospital.

Finally, we must thank for their practical help Dave Kaplan, Soraya Lawrence, Simon Cole and especially Tony Aitman.

Elizabeth Clarke and Richard Peters

January 1990

First Impressions

'THIS IS SOVIET aircraft' was the swift explanation given by the Aeroflot steward as he saw us struggling with the mechanism for releasing the meal tray in front of us. This set the tone for what we were to find from then on – things not working properly, nobody expecting them to and everybody saying as much.

Free copies of *Soviet Weekly* were available to every passenger. They painted a picture of doom and gloom – of problem after problem and of the Communist Party fighting for its life. There was a report of Gorbachev's recent speech on the national question, vainly attempting to hold back the tide of rebellion, emphasised by another headline: 'Lithuania produces independence blueprint'. There were the latest figures on the economy: a budget deficit of more than 100 billion roubles, a severe slowing down in growth rates, 6 per cent of industrial and 16 per cent of retail enterprises showing a loss, 6 million unemployed and over 800 employment offices newly created. One article was entitled 'Shop supplies to be boosted by 35 billion roubles'. Elsewhere: 'Over 2 million man hours have been wasted so far this year because of strikes.'

This Soviet aircraft may have been cramped and scruffy, but it brought us safely into Leningrad. The airport is dark, dingy and thronged by down-at-heel taxi-drivers, people wanting to change money and many ordinary working citizens waiting for friends and family.

A dilapidated taxi commissioned by the state agency Intourist (through whom everything has had to be booked) takes us slowly over chronically pot-holed roads. In the dark, we pass colossal buildings – huge blocks of workers' flats, massive factories working late belching out what the taxi driver sarcastically calls 'clean air'.

This is a city of 6 million workers. Neon lights proclaim the 'heroism' of the city, the 'true worth of labour' and similar slogans. These strike you at first as a pleasant change from the garish commercial advertising of the capitalist world. If you close your eyes to the hypocrisy of the ruling elite, it is almost acceptable. But you soon find how unacceptable *all* the slogans of the bureaucracy have become.

We pass the massive building of the Winter Palace, stormed in 1917. The taxi driver points out the battleship *Aurora* in the distance, the Peter and Paul Fortress and the Finland Station – 'where Lenin arrived in 1917'. A little further away is the Smolny Institute, where Lenin declared that the first ever workers' government 'must now proceed to construct the socialist order.'

At the hotel, we are brought face to face with the seamier side of Soviet life. We are immediately approached for changing money and buying up black market goods. We are put into accommodation which does not seem anything like value for the vast sums we have been forced to pay in advance. A school party from Britain is bothered all night by *fartsovshiki* (spivs) knocking at their doors. The atmosphere in the hotel is horrible. Alcohol is available for hard currency in the night club, and the place seems to play the role of a glorified brothel.

On the Nevsky Prospect

The next day, we set out to get our bearings. First a long and bumpy journey into town by bus. The fare is minimal – five kopecks (five pence). Walking towards the famous Nevsky Prospect, we pass by the 'Engineer's Castle'.Built by Tsar Paul I, like a medieval fortress, it had failed to protect him from his enemies who grew more numerous as his regime grew harsher. He was smothered to death in his bed by conspirators under the instructions of the Governor-General of St Petersburg. We cannot help but draw parallels with Gorbachev's position. No doubt he wishes he could surround himself with fortifications. Is he doomed to be removed by a hard liner such as Ligachev or Gidaspov, or will the masses take things into their own hands?

A lot of people are out and about now and the Nevsky Prospect is crowded. The inevitable queues have formed for the shops, which are open on Sundays. The biggest one we see forms suddenly, apparently out of thin air. It involves young and old, soldiers and sailors in their uniforms, and turns out to be . . . for a special kind of ice cream!

Our impression of the crowd is that it is overwhelmingly proletarian. There is more variety in people's clothes than we remember from the late '60s or '70s – more colour. But in general, life seems to be grey, drab, sparse, hard. It is lit up only by simple delights – special ice cream, the warm company of friends, a carnation or two from the flower seller at the Metro or the appearance on the streets of something new, or even something banned. But this is to become evident only later.

Today, we see groups of people huddle around outdoor artists, some of whom turn out to be selling opposition literature as well as their portraits and pictures. We pass the crossing of Nevsky Prospect with another broad boulevard where one of the most memorable scenes of the revolution was captured on film: a mass demonstration scattered under fire from the military.

We are curious to know what everyone is thinking, what their lives feel like, whether many of them have been involved in any kind of protests against the regime. We are uncertain about approaching them, partly because of the language, partly because we still don't know how 'open' the situation is.

Unable this first day to track down any of the people whose names and addresses we have, we at least acquaint ourselves with some of the practicalities of life like how to get food and tea and how to telephone. It costs the equivalent of two pence for a three minute phone call, less than £1 for a two course meal with tea.

We see people looking at little hand-written notices posted up on derelict buildings or fencing. Most are offering flat-swaps. At the bottom of each is a 'phone number written sideways – 6 or 8 times – and cut into detachable strips. Anybody interested in the flat-swap ... or the maths lesson or the musical instrument ... can tear off the 'phone number, take it home, and get in touch. Judging by the fences full of such 'adverts', there are thousands of families using a little direct action to solve their housing and financial problems.

We came across an old market hall in which co-operators from the countryside had laid out their wares. There didn't seem to be a lot of buying going on. We took some photographs and immediately an old woman started talking to us about the swingeing prices being charged. The pears – very small specimens – were selling for three roubles a kilo. 'They are 20 kopecks in the shops,' she told us, 'but the shops never have any.' Tomatoes are two and a half roubles – '80 kopecks in the shops'. Apples and green beans, likewise.

On another day, we saw parsnips the size of your little finger being snapped up from an impromptu stall outside the tube station. No sign anywhere of bananas, oranges, grapes or other fruit. Potatoes even seem to be in short supply, most meals in restaurants being served with rice or a kind of dumpling or just black bread.

'Life is difficult – yes,' said the old woman in the market, 'but Mikhail Gorbachev has not been there for long only four years. The Russian people are very simple. We put up with everything under Stalin. I lost every member of my family in the war.'

The 'flat-swap' fence

Blockadniks on the November March

In the four-year long blockade of Leningrad that started in 1941, one million people, maybe more, were starved to death. Hundreds of thousands were reduced to eating leather and cardboard. Many froze to death in the snow. Everyone suffered either permanent damage to their health, to their family life or to their sanity. Later, we were to hear how these *Blockadniks* – the people who survived the blockade – had constantly been promised a better deal and had loyally tolerated their lot. After 45 years, they were still expected to live in cramped 'temporary' accommodation on a pittance of a pension. And now things were getting worse, instead of better. On the unofficial demonstration on 7 November, these old people would march proudly and defiantly behind their own banner – but this is to leap ahead! On this first Sunday of our visit, we see only a little disturbance back on the Nevsky. It looks like a demonstration moving along the pavement amongst the crowds. Could this be some political activity? It turns out to be a group of tambourine-waving Hari-Krishna fanatics! It certainly attracts attention. They leave a wake of curious, surprised and amused faces behind them as they go. A little disappointed, we console ourselves by noting that even this is a sign of the 'opening up' of society. Not long ago, no doubt, these people would have been arrested for anti-Soviet activities and 'put away'!

The Leningrad Unions

The bleakness of our first day rapidly dissolved. The following morning with some trepidation we phoned the leader of one of Leningrad's independent trade unions. He was delighted and wanted to meet us straight away. We waited, wondering nervously whether the powers-that-be who had doubtless listened to our phone call, might get to us before the man we wanted to meet. No such problem!

Vasili beamed and shook our hands warmly. 'This is a decisive moment for our country. There is no going back!' We walked and talked non-stop – through the streets and then in a snack bar – for no less than five hours. We discussed everything and anything.

Vasili drew a number of diagrams on the small pieces of paper that substitute as serviettes to demonstrate the interconnections of all the different layers of the bureaucracy – the soviets, the ministries, the state bodies, the Central Committee. He put figures on how many millions were involved in each layer, and on how much of the cake they consumed. He explained, again in graphic form, the superfluous layers which *Perestroika* was aiming to diminish. As many as 400,000 managers have been removed.

This vast, top-heavy society was grinding to a halt in spite of these reforms, Vasili insisted. The methods of one-party control were too cumbersome and attempts to reorganise in the factories were already leading to an explosion of dissatisfaction.

Vasili told us about his union. We discussed Poland and Solidarity. We discussed 'State Capitalism' – the idea that the bureaucracy is a capitalist class. We discussed Gorbachev's reforms that had actually created more problems – disruption, shortages, inflation. There had been great hopes and poor results. When the lid had been lifted, workers had moved, often in the name of Gorbachev. Then they had seen the limits to his support for their aims. On paper, yes . . . Gorbachev has more power and positions than Stalin. His party is still the party of the bureaucracy.

Lessons of Poland

On a number of occasions, we were to find the recent experience of *Solidarity*'s evolution was salutary. It was obvious that the emerging independent trade unions in the Soviet Union look to the *Solidarity* of 1980-81 – the mass movement of ten million workers, the fighting organisation built to defend workers' rights, wages and conditions. But when *Solidarity* had begun to challenge the very rule of the bureaucracy, it had been crushed.

'That's how it could be with us,' Vasili was quick to comment, but he seemed undaunted by the way in which things had developed in Poland. The leadership of *Solidarity* had opposed strikes, gone into the government and way over 'to the capitalist road'. The Polish bureaucracy, he agreed, still had control of the armed bodies of men through the ministries of Defence and Interior, and the *Solidarity* regime was obviously heading for crisis. Vasili could not condone the fact that Walesa was now living in Millionaires' Row, either. Nevertheless, he preferred to turn a deaf ear to our criticisms. He simply did not want to believe the worst of what had gone wrong in Poland. His union had written to Walesa inviting him to come to Leningrad, but they had heard nothing.

Vasili was clearly determined to retain intact his faith that a serious challenge to the rule of the bureaucracy could not only be mounted, but could succeed. He is a stubborn man in the best sense of the word, dedicated to the building of a powerful, mass, independent trade union organisation. Along with others, he had started out with a campaign to democratise the official state unions.

Now, they had concluded that this was no longer viable. In effect, they have put up a 'sign board'. They have made a courageous 'declaration of intent'. They are convinced that workers will gain confidence in their own strength on the basis of events and on the basis of the struggles they are involved in. They will fill out the independent trade unions into mass organisations.

Many of the big factories in Leningrad have got semi-permanent 'Strike Committees', which have been involved in leading skirmishes and strike struggles on a number of occasions in the recent period. The managers were involved in the official workers' committees (STKs), but the workers did not want them in their organisations. The members of Vasili's union could see enormous wastage and expense in carrying the vast administrative apparatus. Many of them felt that the solution to the problems of the economy lay with increasing wages, but this brought them straight up against the problems of productivity and of incentives to work. In Vasili's opinion, more money was needed to be put into productive capacity, rather than sustaining a vast army of officials and bureaucrats – a view we were to hear repeatedly.

Vasili had the idea that the bureaucrats could be seen as 'state capitalists'. They live the life-style of capitalists. Nevertheless, we argued, the state still owns the means of production. The bureaucrats are managers and 'superintendents' over the planned economy. But they have usurped political power and receive vastly inflated wages – far more than those of mere superintendents. The crises in the economy, we maintained, are not those endemic in capitalist society of over-production, of the blind play of productive forces. Nor are they even solely crises of under-production. So much is produced that never reaches the people or the factories that require the products.

The problems of production stem from a persisting chronically low rate of productivity. Apart from insufficient investment in modern technology, there is also a lethargy, a neglect that arises from decades of exclusion from decision-making at all levels.

What exists now in the Stalinist states is a crisis of bureaucratic mismanagement that only a programme of workers' democracy can overcome. We had already come to this conclusion from afar but here it was to be irrefutably confirmed to us daily.

In the summer, Vasili and his union received a message of solidarity from the workers' Labour MP for Broadgreen, Terry Fields. It was printed in full in the union's journal – an illegal or 'unofficial' publication but with a 2,000 circulation in 10 different cities. We went over many of the points in the letter with Vasili – (see appendix).

11

We then talked a little of Liverpool's great fight against the Tories. But the snack bar was closing. As we went out onto the street, Vasili asked us about Liverpool's tragedy at the Hillsborough football match. There had been many similar disasters in the Soviet Union, hushed up sometimes for years. We told him of the campaign by Marxists in Liverpool against the Football Association, the police, the government and the 'kept' press that had attempted to slander the fans and Liverpool itself. Newsagents had dropped Murdoch's newspaper, the *Sun*, in disgust and some replaced it with the *Militant* because of its stance on the Hillsborough disaster.

We accompanied Vasili as he made his way to see someone who worked for the television. He had been promised a chance to publicise the union. At first, we questioned what seemed to us a reckless step to take. Weren't Vasili's forces still too small to throw down a challenge against such a powerful apparatus? But this was not the first, and by no means the last, surprise in store for us. We had to adjust rapidly. How different things were from what we had imagined!

Before he left us, Vasili gave us copies of his union's journal. It is produced, like all the 'unofficial' newspapers, in the Baltic states. It is illegal to organise, yet organisations are mushrooming. It is illegal to print independent papers, yet they abound! The situation is *far more* open than we had anticipated. We had already stopped assuming that everyone standing or sitting near us was a KGB man. But, just as we thought it was safe to be talking the way we were, walking beside a canal that borders Leningrad's 'Summer Gardens', Vasili stopped to allow a man with the proverbial hat and briefcase to go reluctantly past us!

We parted with Vasili as with an already close friend. We turned from the ornate gateway at the Neva end of the gardens back towards the wide open space of the Mars Field. This famous meeting place is bordered by the barracks of the Pavlovski Guards.

In February 1917, the soldiers of this regiment were among the first to turn their guns against the Tsarist government. A memorial was built in 1919 to the martyrs of that year of revolution and those of the Civil War and, on May Day of 1920, 16,000 people took part in a *subotnik* – a day of voluntary labour – to beautify the square around it. Now, an eternal flame burns in the middle of it. Newly-wed couples come straight to the monument from the registry office in their finery to lay bunches of flowers in memory of the fallen class warriors. Lunacharsky's verses on the four gateways to the monument brim with a sense of history, pride in the great heroes and a supreme optimism in the spread of world revolution against tyranny.

That evening, we see Gorbachev chairing the televised deliberations of the Supreme Soviet. He has a surprisingly casual manner. The discussion is on the role of the new committees of workers and their relations to the trade unions. Some interesting points are obviously made, but no radical changes are forthcoming on the new trade union law. On the news, they declare that 25 billion roubles worth of food is rotting in the railway sidings – confirmation of our point about production and supply! Distribution is literally bogged down by mismanagement. An item on co-ops in Czechoslovakia indicates that only 40 per cent of earnings of the enterprises are used for wages. One of the complaints of many workers we were to meet was that, under the state plan, far too little of each enterprise's earnings was available for wages.

Each night on TV there is a spot for publicly shaming antisocialist elements! Yesterday a woman was being humiliated in front of the masses for stealing jewellery and money. She broke down in tears. Tonight it is the turn of a man dealing in narcotics! In the next five weeks, we were to see the news on television probably only twice more, so busy did life become!

The workers' leaders meet

THROUGHOUT OUR VISIT, we met groups with newspapers and full-timers living on the edge of legality. There were organisations drawing up programmes, issuing declarations, organising conferences, travelling to other republics, meeting up with lefts from America, from Britain, from France etc.

We were indeed 'late' on the scene, as Dmitri commented when we first met him: 'What's kept you?'

This man was already devoting himself 12 hours a day to producing a journal, building an independent workers' organisation, discussing with this person, that person, preparing material, studying, selling his paper . . .

In an interview with a Swedish journalist, the day we first met him, Dmitri explained that he was a 'non-person'. His step-father was Jewish and had been pushed out of his job. His mother was also being victimised at work, so they had both left the country. Dmitri himself was all set to follow. Then he saw the political situation dramatically and rapidly changing and he made the decision to stay and fight. (He had spent two years in jail for refusing to go into the army because of the Afghan war.)

He told the journalist that he envisaged an 'umbrella' organisation like the Leningrad Popular Front developing into a mass movement and the new, independent trade unions taking on flesh rapidly in the future. Later he told us he thought the official party – the Communist Party – could even split. Gorbachev could lead a section away. Neither the Party nor the official unions, in his opinion, were susceptible to democratic change from within.

He and some close friends were keen to hear what we had to say – what social forces we based ourselves on, what ideas we had of the past, present and future of the USSR and what we could do to assist in their struggle. Again, 'What do you think of *Solidarity*?' and 'What is your opinion of the Popular Fronts?'

We had expected to listen rather than put forward our opinions at this early stage, but we nevertheless found our basic analysis

14

readily accepted. Historic developments were taking place. The miners' strike had transformed the situation so that things would never be the same: they had sensed their power and demonstrated the strength of the mighty working class that now had such a predomination in society. These activists accept that, when the movement develops from below, the bureaucracy will fight for its life and it will be a vicious struggle. They knew of Trotsky's analogy, that the bureaucracy would not allow its claws to be removed one by one.

The enemy is powerful, we insisted. Time is short. In the summer, all the wings of the bureaucracy had come together in the face of the mass movement of the working class. Even Boris Yeltsin had argued against strike action.

This last point Dmitri, Pyotr and Vasili were not sure of. They also questioned our claim that the proletariat of the USSR is the most educated and cultured in the world. The longer we stayed, the more we were impressed with the large numbers of people who could read and speak fluently languages of countries which they could never visit. We met many people who knew more about the literature of our country than many of our fellow citizens. We heard people not only waxing lyrical about their much-loved poet Pushkin, but reciting long extracts. We saw many people reading, many visiting the theatre and the ballet. We met physicists, chemists, biologists with great interest in the application of their sciences to benefit society, but . . . that is not the whole story!

Our friends firstly had no direct knowledge, and therefore may have had an exaggerated view, of the level of education and culture in capitalist countries, which in general has deteriorated recently through drastic cuts in public spending. Secondly, they are no doubt appalled at the stifling of talent they witness daily – the bureaucratic, formalistic approach to education, the lack of development of ideas and inventions and the failure to apply even the technology that has been developed in the interests of the population as a whole. We were to find a deep-seated resentment, not only at the stunted growth of the abilities of the ordinary person, but also of the potential of society as a whole. It is a keenly felt indignity for an aware and cultured people to be denied access to books, to newspapers, to information, not only of what is happening internationally but even in their own country.

With a few minor interruptions – people going in and out – the discussion proceeded. We were asked where we thought the struggle for democratic rights fitted in with the struggle for workers' democracy. The first task of Marxists is to defend and fight for democratic rights, we maintained. Even where they exist on paper, only a mass movement can force their implementation. The struggle for democratic rights inevitably begs the question of the right of the present regime to rule in the name of the working class. As the workers move on that issue, they will confront the bureaucratic caste and move to throw off its dictatorship over them. The mass movement itself was already driving a coach and horses through the restrictions on the right to strike.

We touched on the re-emergence of the national question. It will enormously complicate the struggle. A state of virtual civil war exists in the Nagorno-Karabakh region. The Baltic states are edging more and more towards secession and the parties of these republics are already trying to break from the central party structure. Gorbachev, we were sure, would be unable to find a solution on the basis of bureaucratic rule. In spite of his protestations, we said that he could be forced to repress the national movement with force. This was three months before Gorbachev sent tanks into Baku!

Mass movements that will develop on the common social problems of all workers can cut across national divisions, but a skilful and sensitive programme on the national question is as important to the success of the political revolution as it was to the success of the revolution of 1917. The nascent workers' movement must uphold the rights of self-determination up to and including secession, but argue none the less for the unity of the working class across all borders. A genuine free and democratic socialist federation in which all language and cultural rights would be respected would pose no threat to any ethnic group.

A growing movement

Dmitri and his friends were modest about their own strength at this stage and about the involvement of the Leningrad proletariat in the opposition movement. There were so many small strikes taking place in the factories and workplaces of Leningrad that it was impossible to cover them all in the papers of the independent trade union movement.

Yet, Pyotr was to insist to us on many occasions, 'The movement is still a baby. It cannot be yet forced to take the giant steps that will be needed in the future.'

Vasili believed that the miners' movement had been extremely political, but was now restricting itself to very limited and simple demands on the economic questions. As he and we would in fact see in the coming weeks, the miners, if anything, were becoming *more* political. The miners of Vorkuta in particular are now looked to by all as the standard-bearers of the fight against the party dictatorship.

We were to return to many of the questions touched on at this meeting. This was just a beginning! Pyotr walked and talked with us, keen to hear what was happening in Britain, and France and Spain. Why had the *Militant* been thrown out of the Labour Party? What were Thatcher's chances of staying in power? He told us numerous anecdotes as we ate, drank coffee and walked with him.

Jokes about shortages and starvation are rife. 'Can you go by horse to Moscow from Leningrad?' 'Yes, unless they eat the horse at Kalinin (a town half-way)!'

Many commodities are sold through the workplace. Even then it is through the drawing of lots. Pyotr told us of a workplace with 800 women, where 42 pairs of women's boots became available. 'You don't know what size they are but if you draw a winning ticket you buy the boots. Then you sell them if they are no good to you! One woman made enough on a pair of boots to buy a giant gateau for her whole department!'

'Why is soap in such short supply?' we asked Pyotr. He laughed. 'That is the question of questions! Professors and academics of all kinds have been conducting interviews and research in all corners of the economy! Why a shortage of soap? As yet no satisfactory explanation. And still a shortage.' On our return to London we found an article in the *Wall Street Journal* two pages long which recounted a whole chain of ministerial bungling and zig-zags which had led to the soap crisis. Workers' control and workers' management would have put soap of all kinds into the shops in a matter of days!

Pyotr told us there is a street in the south of Leningrad called 'Strike' Street, named after the numerous struggles that took place in that area in the years leading up to the great revolution. However, during the Polish events of 1980-81 when strikes were never reported in the Soviet press and were only referred to as 'temporary interruptions to work', 'Strike' Street rapidly became known as 'Temporary-interruption-to-work' Street!

According to Pyotr, many of Trotsky's writings are now available. Extracts have appeared in the official press and other works are circulating through unofficial channels. Many of the ideas we have explained, Pyotr says, are widely held. But so many of Lenin's slogans, he cautions, have been completely discredited. They used to display them everywhere. Not so much now! To many people, 'every cook should be able to be prime minister', for example, has been completely discredited by the bureaucracy. What cook has ever made it to prime minister, after all – although a few prime ministers have nevertheless been forced to become cooks!

Lenin and Democracy

Another activist we visit lives near 'Uprising Square'. His mother plies us with coffee, cake and apples, making a fuss of her English visitors. Valentin was recently detained for two weeks for running a stall of unofficial literature in the street.

He has a vast library of revolutionary literature. He admires Marx and Engels but he admires Solzhenitzyn too! He is interested in Trotsky but cannot forgive Lenin for the dissolution of the Constituent Assembly in 1918! We countered with the argument that Lenin was, if anything, over generous on this score.

Elections for the Assembly went ahead on 12 November 1917. The Bolsheviks won overwhelming support in the working class centres, but, on the basis of the provinces, the right wing of the Social Revolutionary Party won a majority in the Assembly, through their support mainly from the richer peasants in areas where the revolution was only just beginning. After the October revolution, they adopted the position of the Cadets – the Constitutional Democrats – and supported the interests of the landowners against the movement of the poor peasants, who were attempting to take over the land.

Right wing SRs claimed that their electoral victory made them the genuine representatives of the people, but the election results lagged way behind the real development of events. The SR leaders had made common cause with the leaders of the counter-revolution who were already preparing to carry through a bloody reaction. The workers and the exploited masses, already involved in the process of social transformation, regarded the soviets as **their** organs. The dispersal of the Assembly on the second day of its meeting early in 1918 was regarded with indifference by politically active workers and poor peasants.

Through the soviets of workers, the most direct democracy in history was being exercised. The frequent election of delegates to these committees was supplemented by the right of recall. As in the Paris Commune, no representative was allowed to receive more than the average skilled wage. The Soviets had combined legislative functions – decision-making – with executive – the carrying out of decisions. The forces of reaction used the Constituent Assembly as a vehicle to begin to plot the downfall of the new Soviet State.

It was dissolved to prevent it from carrying out its undemocratic, counter-revolutionary role.

Before we leave Valentin, he gives us newspapers and *samizdats* galore, but warns us it is illegal to take any printed matter – even official newspapers – out of the country! We promised to send him some of our material and hoped it would reach him.

At an independent trade union meeting

The meeting that evening of a Leningrad independent union was no hole-in-the-corner affair – hardly a secret meeting. This 'clandestine' organisation openly booked a room under its own name in a well-known 'House of Culture'. It was a vast building, with theatres, meeting-rooms, coffee bars – teeming with life, teeming with Komsomol (Young Communist League) and Party members, teeming with Popular Front members and . . . independent trade union members! The main stairway was dominated by a vast portrait of Lenin speaking to the masses.

As we waited for the allocated room to be unlocked, we spoke to a woman who pleaded with us to tell the people of Britain what the situation was like for women in so-called 'soviet' society. They suffer long hours of drudgery at work, long hours of drudgery at home, long hours in the queues. In her opinion, they are permanently treated as second-class citizens, if not, more crudely, as domestic slaves.

'Can you put us in touch with feminists in London?' 'Certainly. We recognise the special problems of women, and can send material produced by working-class women in Britain striving for reforms and for the socialist transformation of society. The extent of the problems you mention are a sure sign that society here is still a million miles from socialism.'

No more than three other women attend the meeting, which starts with around 40, expands to 45 and then to 50. People arrive late for the meeting, make a speech and disappear! They may return after a smoking break, while others go out for a chat and a cigarette. There is constant movement. In fact the whole meeting shifts from one room to another because it has got too big.

Workers' leaders speak of their struggles. A woman from the Post Office (actually a prominent member of the official trade union, we find out later) outlines all the issues that are bubbling up at her workplace. She speaks as rapidly as machine-gun fire. The situation is going to lead to a head-on clash. Action will have to be taken. Tens of thousands of workers are involved.

A power worker from the Vyborg district stands up to explain to the Post Office worker how, in his recent strike, they came directly up against the Party bureaucracy. 'The Party decides what is spent and how it is spent and where the proceeds of any labour are distributed. Hence, if you fight for a bigger share you will not only be taking illegal action, but you will be risking dismissal from your work.' This must not be allowed to stop anyone, he insists; but it explains why, as yet, just a handful of leaders will be organised. The mass of workers are prepared to take action and are prepared to support their 'strike committee' representatives but they are not yet prepared to identify themselves as members of an illegal organisation.

The 'business' session of the meeting proceeds at a gallop. Then, as apparently anarchically as it has proceeded, it suddenly comes to a stop! It is the turn of the visitors from Britain. Other business can be taken later on or at the next Wednesday's meeting. The union meets twice a week.

We set out our ideas of what was happening in their country:

'Life for most workers, as we can see for ourselves, is becoming intolerable. Even the most basic necessities are in short supply. The air, the water of the lakes and rivers are poisoned. The health and safety of men, women and children is daily at risk. This is not socialism (approving voices). This is not what so many gave their lives for. Until now there has been a sense of powerlessness in the face of the state that at last is beginning to crumble. The miners' strike has marked a turning-point.

'The establishment of independent trade unions is an absolute necessity to take the struggle forward. We salute the valiant efforts of the comrades here ... The road will not be easy but the revolutionary threads of the past are being retied. In the context of an economy with a budget deficit of 120 billion roubles, the struggle for a bar of soap, for fresh fruit and vegetables, for meat or for an extra few days' holiday, for a shorter working week and a living wage, is bound up with the struggle for democratic rights. These demands bring into full focus the urgent need for the right to organise, the right to strike, the right to meet freely, the right to a free press, to free elections and for the right of all parties to stand in elections ...

'Our programme in Britain is for a 35-hour week; £150 a week minimum wage; for the fullest democracy inside the trade unions and the Labour Party; for the taking into public ownership of the major monopolies on the basis of workers' control and management. Marxists are at the head of a mass movement in Scotland to defy the Tory government. Millions in Britain as a whole will refuse to pay a new tax, imposed to once again rob the poor to pay to the rich!'

The workers listen intently and we conclude:

'We have been chided for leaving it so long before coming to your country. Let's hope we can make up for lost time, and build for the victory of socialism on an international scale. For that we can take no better slogan than: "Workers of all countries unite"!'

Questions, questions, questions

First the appreciation, then the questions in rapid succession! 'What is your organisation?' 'What are your relations with the Communist Party?' 'Do you have links with *Solidarity*?' 'What are your differences with *Solidarity*?' 'When you say workers' democracy what do you mean by workers?' 'Did you support the London Underground workers' strike?' 'Did they win?' 'If strikes are declared illegal should workers go on strike?' 'Are you for public ownership – state or collective?' Each question had to be answered immediately – no time to reflect!

'What is the minimum wage in Britain?' 'What is the average wage?' 'What is the cost of living?' 'Do capitalists do anything?'(!) 'Do you have ordinary workers in your country?'

When you are then asked point-blank before a meeting of workers' leaders, who daily risk dismissal and imprisonment for their activities, 'Who do you see as the main enemy?' and 'Why have you not been before?', you cannot fudge the issue!

'The main enemy is the capitalist class in the West and the ruling bureaucracy in the East.' 'We have not been earlier because the country has been ruled by a military police dictatorship . . . and still is!' As you raise your eyebrows and throw a glance towards the door, some of the workers present probably realise you think you could be arrested at any moment. But a few of them have done a spell 'inside' and anticipate doing more, so . . . we're all in this together!

The meeting reluctantly accepts it must draw to a close. There are many more questions where those already asked have come from. Every answer has been eagerly snapped up and rapidly digested. Things are moving fast in this country and solutions are being sought in every direction.

This union meeting discussed standing a candidate in the regional elections. It has discussed its links with the People's Front, a forthcoming conference, and what letters to send to the Supreme Soviet.

The comrade in the chair thanks us and pledges his union will maintain links with Terry Fields' campaign. 'The main thing,' he declares, 'is building the union. There has been much talk of Lenin tonight but he was not in favour of independent trade unions!' We had to protest that Vladimir Ilyich was, on the contrary, in favour of independent trade unions. Lenin had insisted on the need for workers to have their own trade unions, to both protect the workers' state, but also to defend themselves against any excessive demands on the part of that state. 'When there is time, maybe we can discuss the issue further. For now, we wish you every success in building your organisation.'

When the meeting did eventually finish there was no rush for the doors. On the contrary, we were gently mobbed. There was no hostility; there were grim faces but no hostility. The anarchists were extremely polite. 'Excuse me, do you mind if we ask you a question? Are there any anarcho-syndicalists in London? . . . We were very interested in what you have to say. We support everyone, including people from other organisations.'

A scientific worker asks us if there is a place for scientists in our scheme of things – do they count as workers? We had to explain on a number of occasions that experts – technicians and scientists – are vital to developing production and society. But, in a workers' state, they should be subject to control by the workforce and not by the local representatives of the bureaucratic elite. We meet a woman from Vladivostok, a victimised teacher with a petition to take to the Supreme Soviet. 'Come and visit me' she says! 'Next time maybe!' (We find out later, foreigners are not allowed to visit Vladivostok anyway.)

An artist member of the union insists we go to his studio and 'discuss with my friends in the shipyards.' Someone with a tape-recorder (who has recorded everything!) tells us he is homeless. Between 10 and 12 per cent of Leningrad's population has no accommodation, he says. 'There are also many unemployed.' 'Come to our meeting tomorrow night.' 'Are you coming to the Popular Front conference at the weekend?' 'What is your newspaper? Can you send us copies?' Our feet are not going to touch the ground! We will have our work cut out to follow up all the opportunities we now have to discuss with people.

What kind of Marxism?

A deep-seated antipathy to Marxism is expressed by a number of workers. So much has been crammed down their throats – so many bits and extracts and distortions. All agree on the need for workers' democracy, but not for the 'dictatorship of the proletariat'. But what else is workers' democracy if not precisely the dictatorship of the proletariat?

What was already becoming clear to us was that not only was the planned economy running into enormous difficulties, but the consciousness of the proletariat, whose historic task is to rescue society from the rule of the bureaucracy in the USSR, had been thrown back a long way. We had to scrap any illusion we might have had that the level of the 'Soviet' worker would be advanced, and that support for the ideas of Lenin, if not of Trotsky because of the criminal handiwork of the Stalinist bureaucracy, would have been far deeper and more widespread. We had to bear in mind that openness – *Glasnost* – had brought into public glare a whole catalogue of ghastly crimes perpetrated by Stalin, but in the name of Lenin and the October revolution. Soviet commentators now estimate that between 30 and 40 million perished. Memories of fascism and world war had been used for decades to prevent a revolt against Stalin or any of his heirs.

The East German Stalinist regime of the past used the crimes of fascism to intimidate the population in a different way. They were made to feel personally guilty and to bend to the yoke to build a new society that could atone for the sins of the past. The bureaucracy in the USSR succeeded for a time in doing the same sort of thing. As the crimes of Stalin could no longer be hidden, even new generations were made to feel that their own parents and grandparents had been too cowardly to rise up and stay the hand of Stalin. Now there are some, particularly older workers, unnerved by the uncertainties of life under Gorbachev, who have convinced themselves that life was better under Stalin. To them, at least the economy was going forward in those days and strict order was maintained, even if some harsh methods had been used.

It is on this layer that people like Nina Andreyevna and the hardliners will depend to whip up support for a return to the iron fist. As the country plunges into what they would call 'chaos', they will sing the praises of 'order', 'centralisation', 'discipline' etc. The open justification of the crimes of Stalin, pronounced by Andreyevna in 1988, acted, as we were to see, as a whip that goaded 'progressive' workers and intellectuals into further efforts to organise opposition to the ruling clique.

We found a peculiar situation in the Soviet Union – the rejection of everything connected with the hated ruling bureaucracy on the part of wide layers of the proletariat and the intelligentsia. This applied not just to the ideas of Marxism – distorted versions of which they had been forced to accept almost from birth. On numerous occasions our descriptions of the horrors of life under capitalism were not believed, they were so like the propaganda of the regime. We had great difficulty in convincing the workers at this meeting and many others that millions were suffering, not only in the third world, but in the so-called advanced capitalist countries. Redundancies and mass unemployment in the West have been continually used as sticks to intimidate the workers of the Stalinist states. They would not believe, either, that people, young and old, lived in cardboard boxes on the streets of London. It was partly a case, too, of not wanting to believe it, now that they were convinced that some other system must be better than what they had got. The absence of clear scientific explanations as to what had gone wrong in society, has created a hiatus, a vacuum, into which has flooded a host of alien ideas. To use an analogy of Trotsky, many have discarded the clothes handed on to them by their parents, only to 'ransack' the wardrobes of their grand-parents and great grand-parents!

We were to have further thoughts on this issue, but it was obvious from this meeting that many workers were searching for a revolutionary alternative to *Perestroika*.

'Freedom of speech, press and assembly'

The Leningrad opposition demonstration.

The 'Democratic Union'

WE WERE INVITED to a meeting of the Democratic Union, an organisation which is continually defying the authorities, flouting the law and condemning the regime. We had read about it in Britain, and it seemed to be virulently anti-communist, but we wanted to see for ourselves. The members we met seemed predominantly young, energetic and idealistic. At least 100 of their comrades had recently been arrested and detained. They are not allowed to use any public buildings. So this Leningrad 'co-ordinating committee' was crowded into a small, hot flat.

Each person present was held to account for their activities over the past week and discussions raged over the question of the need for a newspaper and the tactics in relation to the regional elections – to boycott or not to boycott – whether to accept invitations from the Komsomol branch to discuss and to speak.

A report was given of a conference held in Chelyabinsk where the authorities seem to have a more liberal attitude than in other cities. The secretary of the Communist Party was there on the first day and the regional secretary was there on the second day. The Popular Front is actually registered as a political party in that city, the only place in the country where that was the case, according to these people. Even monarchists from Siberia had attended! We thought everything was going surprisingly well when they talked of a day school to discuss the theory of Lenin and when they spoke enthusiastically about the committees in the factories known as 'Committees for Preparing for Strikes'.

This group was extremely disciplined. They had a discussion about membership and 'candidate membership' and they also took to task anyone who hadn't set up their stall on the Saturday morning in the main squares – an activity which quite often brought them 10 days' or two weeks' imprisonment!

Back to Kerensky?

But we noticed everyone was using the old name for the city, 'Petrograd', or even 'Petersburg'! They listened intently to a lengthy taped message of a 'phone call from Moscow. They discussed a demonstration planned for 30 October – Political Prisoners' Day – and another one in opposition to the official anniversary celebrations on 7 November. Last year, a whole demonstration of theirs was arrested. In August, they had further problems with the authorities – hardly surprising since they were demonstrating for a return to the regime of February 1917 under the flag of the Kerensky republic! They discussed plans for open-air activities, stalls etc, and finally gave us the floor.

As yet unaware of the depth of their hatred not only of the regime but of 'communism', we introduced ourselves as Marxists in the British Labour Party and trade unions, supporters of the newspaper, *Militant*. We spoke of solidarity and workers' democracy and of perspectives. 'During the miners' strike, as we understand it, the committees swept away the old guard, banned alcohol, took over the policing of the communities, reduced crime to almost nothing and generally felt in charge of society. A new way of running things had developed that almost ousted the old power. Nevertheless, there is still no mass alternative to participation in elections. They should be used as a platform. We would fight for workers' representatives on workers' wages.' We spoke of the political revolution and our programme. Then, at the mention of Lenin, the dam burst! One of the assembled company stood up and walked out in disgust and others prepared to follow.

We finished with the capitalists of the world. They were crowing that they had 'won'. Gorbachev had played into their hands, but had indicated the bureaucracy's total lack of confidence by asking Greenspan, head of the US Federal Reserve, to come to Moscow to give advice. The tables would be turned as the recession set in! . . .

Then the howling began!

The 'great' October Revolution had been a 'coup', unsupported by the mass of the population! Lenin had led directly to Stalin, Trotsky too – the suppression of the Kronstadt rising in 1921 proved this conclusively! Lenin's democratic centralism meant that if you arrived late for a meeting, you were imprisoned! Lenin had been against democratic centralism, etc., etc.

We countered each of these arguments. No socialist revolution can be carried through without the involvement of the masses. The Bolsheviks had won a majority in the Soviets by the time of the insurrection. Kerensky had been dragging the peasant and proletarian masses further and further into war and famine. Under the leadership of Lenin and Trotsky, the October Revolution had brought numerous oppressed peoples into the modern world.

Lenin had warned against bureaucratism and the rise of Stalin. Trotsky had conducted a life-long struggle against 'socialism in one country', and against the elimination of Bolshevism and its adherents. He had explained the objective reasons for the rise of Stalin. In an article *Hue and Cry over Kronstadt*, Trotsky explained the material basis for the rising in 1921 and the reasons that necessitated its swift suppression. A widespread discontent had developed amongst the middle class, especially the rural petit bourgeoisie – the peasants – with the harsh regime of War Communism. This was seized on by representatives of the defeated classes. If allowed to proceed, this uprising would have provided a bridgehead for counter-revolution. Trotsky's writings refute every one of the anarchist slanders of the time now echoed by latter-day know-nothings who seek to use these events as 'proof' of the use by Lenin and Trotsky of the same kind of terrorist methods to suppress dissent as those used by Stalin on a gigantic scale in later years.

If the Kronstadt revolt had been successful, it would have led to the liquidation of all the social gains of the revolution, both from the Soviet Union itself and the rest of the world. (For further clarification, see *Kronstadt* by VI Lenin and Leon Trotsky).

Lenin and Trotsky had been in favour of democratic centralism, in fact they had found it the most effective way to build a revolutionary party. They insisted that it meant the maximum of democracy and discussion and that the centralism needed at times of crisis stemmed from the authority of a leadership tried and tested over a period of time. (What it never meant was being imprisoned for being late to meetings!)

Much of the meeting had left the flat by the time the arguments began to fly. The most interested members continued the discussion – the argument, the friendly banter – down the stairway, into the street, onto the Metro.

One of these people had been victimised. Another had given up his job in order to work for a change in society. At present, they are going in the wrong direction; some are obviously convinced counter- revolutionaries. There are people who risk imprisonment to sell banned books like Bolgakov's *White Guard*. But after the liquidation of millions in the name of the October Revolution, and decades of lies and distortions in the official media, it is not surprising if everything that the regime stands for, or says it stands for, is rejected.Their actions have nurtured illusions in the idea that 'If only we had stopped the clock at February 1917, and tried to develop on the basis of capitalism, with capitalist democracy, perhaps we would have been in a better situation today.' Amongst the best workers' leaders, such ideas will be burnt out by the experience of the struggle itself. Also, when the present boom in the West exhausts itself, the glow and glitter will disappear from the picture of capitalism.

Even the official press, for example a *Moscow News* item on 1917, gives credence to this idea that 'if only' . . . If only the alliance of all the forces against the attempted counter- revolutionary coup led by General Kornilov in the summer of 1917 could have been maintained for a period, perhaps the 'unpleasantness' that followed the revolution could have been avoided!

Some who call themselves Marxists, even 'Trotskyists', failed to give a fully rounded out explanation for the rise of Stalinism. They correctly point to the failure of the revolution to spread to the West, to the backwardness of the economy, the exhaustion and lack of experience of the working class and to the intervention by 21 imperialist armies. But then they give effect as cause! They say that the workers of Western Europe were moving towards the revolutionary overthrow of capitalism, but they stopped on the road because they were 'alienated' by the banning of parties and the pushing through of war-communism and the NEP. If the revolution had spread, emergency measures would not have been necessary. If the workers' leaders of just one advanced capitalist country had adopted policies that would have carried the revolution to a successful conclusion, they could have changed the course of history.

Democratic Union members protest, March '89......

......*and are arrested by the KGB*

With the students

ON THE BLEAK, grey afternoon of 13 October, we witnessed the first public demonstration of students since Stalin's rise to power. Accumulating resentment had come to a head on the burning issue of accommodation. It seems that the defence cuts had pushed thousands of soldiers back into full time education and these had been given priority for student housing. Overcrowding had already reached crisis proportions, and students finding their places taken by soldiers had decided to act.

The mood of the youth in the colleges and Universities is so often a barometer that indicates the seething discontent accumulating in the depths of any society. The least prepared to accept privations, injustices and repression and the most prepared to act without thought of their own safety, they take their place in the vanguard of the revolution alongside the youth in the factories.

The students of Leningrad have a proud tradition to follow. The Technological Institute not only housed many a revolutionary student, it was also the scene of the first Petrograd Soviet of Deputies, which met in the Physics auditorium. Trotsky described a scene in 1905 when he addressed a demonstration from the balcony of the University. 'The street was packed with people. The students' blue caps and the red banners were bright spots among the hundred thousand strong crowd.'

This modest demonstration in 1989 was well organised, with loudspeaker equipment rigged up on a vast plinth outside a sports and recreation centre. Speakers from a number of opposition organisations took the microphone. Representatives of Pamyat, the arch-reactionary chauvinistic organisation, had turned up, but were quietly and firmly ostracised. The organisers of the demonstration were obviously disappointed with the turnout, but after decades of a blanket ban on all forms of protest, the first steps would inevitably be modest.

Wanting to know more, we approached some of the students and sheltered with them under their umbrellas. They were eager not only to tell us what kind of conditions they were living in, but to *show* us. When the demonstration began to disperse, they took us in a taxi right across the city to the other side of Leningrad. We finally travelled down what was virtually a dirt track to a bleak tower block standing 29 storeys high amongst other bleak tower blocks. We had passed through mile upon mile of characterless rows of barrack-like workers' apartments. There seemed to be few shops and few lights, also few cars.

Inside the block, Anton showed us the notice he had put up announcing the demonstration. In fact he took it down and gave it to us. When we went up in the lift to his corridor, he told us of a student prank when 30 of them had crammed into one of these lifts which were only supposed to take five!

Treated like guests of honour in Anton's tiny, cramped quarters, we talked and listened and listened and talked. The room filled up to capacity with fellow students, mostly members of his 'block committee'. One student brought in his brother to meet us – a soldier who had served in Afghanistan. We were urged to talk to him about his experiences, but this proved fruitless. Understandably, not having met us before, not knowing who we were, he endeavoured to give the impression that little or no ill feeling existed over the intervention, the conditions that had to be endured and the casualties etc. But you could see from his bearing and demeanour that his experiences had taken their toll. He was a nervous young man. These two had Muslim names, a reminder of the vastness of the country and also of the wide measure of integration. The student who prepared our food was visiting from Karkhov.

Dimya, Karyl, Constantin and Anton are part of a seven-strong committee that has taken over the running of the tower block student hostel. They told us:

'There are masses of rules of behaviour for students in their accommodation and a "commandant" on each floor to ensure they are enforced – a representative of the apparatus. If you break the rules, you are thrown out, not just of your accommodation, but out of college as well. We were fed up with this. We are 560 in our block in these tiny rooms – just big enough for one person (no more than nine feet by twelve). Most rooms have two students in. There are sometimes twenty sharing one kitchen and one toilet! We do everything ourselves - cooking and cleaning in turns. We run things. Incidentally, we are the only block in Leningrad where you can drink vodka in your rooms – because we decide on the rules!' (We sampled some a little later on!)

'We get very small grants: 50-75 roubles per month.' Some other students we met said their grant was 40 roubles and hadn't changed for 20 years! 'We pay 24 roubles per month for our so-called "accommodation". Travel is not expensive – five kopecks a journey by bus, five kopecks per journey by Metro, but we are stuck out in the outskirts of town and have to spend 55 minutes to an hour each way to get to the Institute. (The Lensoviet Institute of Technology). There are 42 colleges in Leningrad, with 250,000 students and we're all dissatisfied with our conditions and with our official union. It does nothing, but it has a lot of resources so we're not sure if we should just pull out and set up independent unions. Maybe we'll do both – try to take over the official union and build independent committees!

'We were disappointed with the turnout today. It was raining, but that's no excuse. Everybody's got to get involved. We've taken the first step. Life is getting more and more difficult. We are only allowed 100 grammes of bathroom soap a month and 400 grammes of household soap, one kilogram of washing powder, one packet of tea (and it's not the best), two kilos of sugar. Take these coupons back with you and show people. We, the students, have to make do with just over three grammes of soap a day and in prison you get seven!

'Outside Moscow and Leningrad, you don't get coupons because there aren't the supplies! Moscow, Leningrad and the Baltics are better looked after and that gives rise to animosities. A lot of things were poured into Siberia after the strike but that was a "one-off".

'The situation led to hoarding. Nobody believes the papers when they say things are not going to be in short supply so, when they see things in the shops, they buy them up. People have money but can't buy the things they need. Tooth paste, tooth brushes, razors, cigarettes, have all been in short supply at various times, so people just buy them because they're afraid supplies will dry up. There was a run on school note-books because no one believed the government when they said there were plenty of them. We don't know what's going to happen; it wasn't clear from today's meeting but we know we've got to fight and organise.

'We're not afraid now. Did you see the stewards – they were special constables, but just wandered about. Before now, we wouldn't have been able to demonstrate like that without being attacked. Things are changing fast and we want to link up, not just in Leningrad, but much further afield. We will be interested in any campaigns you organise and any papers and material you can get us. We know we haven't been told the whole story about some of the leaders of the revolution and we know why.'

In fact, they were quite specific about what had happened with

Trotsky and they knew why he had been persecuted and murdered in the fight against Stalin. They were familiar with some of his ideas, from reading extracts of his material which have been published. They were very keen to know more about his role, his programme and how his ideas could be used today to transform the situation. They would be interested in any of Trotsky's writings that we could furnish them with.

They expressed a common distaste in how Lenin had been 'beatified' - turned into a saint. 'All the statues and pictures of him in Russia show him with Russian features, in Uzbekistan with Uzbeki features, etc., just as they try to do with Jesus Christ.'

One of the students who came from the Ukraine, told us with pride how, in the summer, he had been with the miners outside the 'White House' in the square of his home town, Burianka, in the Donbas. He had sensed for himself the tremendous power that workers could wield in society. It gave him great optimism for the future.

Anton escorted us all the way across Leningrad again to our bus stop. He told us about his father, who was in charge of the building of part of a power station in the Ukraine. Some 'Greens' had organised a protest delegation to Moscow and there was widespread consternation in the area. Memories of Chernobyl, and horror at the ecological disasters sweeping unchecked through the country have since our return brought new mass demonstrations, forcing even the complete cancellation of the building of one radar station.

This Saturday night in Leningrad, Anton waited with us for nearly an hour in the freezing cold, exchanging jokes. Had we heard the one about Brezhnev, when his advisers had told him that the Americans had landed on the Moon?: 'Hmm . . . so the Americans have landed on the Moon? We must get a man on the Sun.' 'Comrade Leonid Ilych, that is impossible! The sun is very hot and it will burn him up!' 'Of course! You are right . . . so we must tell him to go at night!'

Did we know the one about the President of France, the President of the United States and the President of the USSR? They are standing at the top of a mountain above a dangerous ravine and they decide to test their henchmen. The French President takes off a gold ring and throws it into the ravine, calling on his number one bodyguard to go and fetch it for him. 'Oh no, Monsieur le President, I cannot do it. I have a wife and children to think of.'

The American President takes off his watch and throws that into the valley. 'Bring me back my watch,' he orders his number one. 'Oh no, Mr President, sir! It's too dangerous. I have a wife and children to think of.'

The President of the USSR takes a dirty handkerchief out of his pocket, throws it into the ravine. Before he has issued the order, his ace body guard dives into the ravine, catches the handkerchief as it falls and brings it back to the top of the mountain. Very impressed, the other Presidents ask him why he has been so daring? 'Simple, comrades. I have a wife and children to think of!'

Ration tickets

Searching for a programme

BY NOW, WE had acquired a large amount of material that we had to go through. There were papers with accounts of strikes, factory bulletins, more declarations. One journal was publishing extracts from Trotsky's *Revolution Betrayed*. There was a newspaper of the Inter-Regional Group of Deputies (Yeltsin and his supporters) and material produced by the Narodny (Popular) Front of Leningrad. One group was predicting 'World War III by the year 2026-7' and 'the first stage of communism in the year 2053'. Were they serious – or was this a dig at the methods of the regime? The same people were so hostile to intellectuals, that they would not allow them to join their organisation!

Pravda and *Izvestia* are about as exciting as the television news. The most popular papers, like *Argumenti y Facti*, and *Ogonyok*, are virtually impossible to buy on the street. Very soon, you get a feeling of some kind of sensory deprivation and start craving for an English language bourgeois paper!

A tour of the big hotels, the main tourist stands and even the US consulate, yielded nothing more than a copy of the *Morning Star*, which had been published before we had even left Britain!

The US consulate was supposed to have a reading room with foreign newspapers. But, like so many other buildings, much of it was closed for repairs – in *remont* – and the reading room was shut. All that was available were telex print-outs from New York. They consisted mainly of the latest baseball and American football results. The only other 'news' was the report of a general knowledge survey. Most Americans, it found, don't know the difference between the Communist Manifesto and the US Constitution or that Roosevelt was the President during the Depression, etc! The message at the bottom was, 'Make sure your kids over there know their history – we've got a bad enough reputation abroad!'

At the Chernychevsky Metro, near the Consulate, the *Oppositsi* newspaper (of the Inter-regional Group), was posted up on a gate and attracted a much larger crowd than the *Pravda*s and *Izvestia*s on the other side of the station.

The whole area, like many parts of the city, seemed dark and drab. Some shops you couldn't see until you were right beside them – steps go suddenly down into shop doorways. The absence of advertising has its disadvantages; you hardly know where to look when you want to buy something. Other shops you cannot miss, by the massive queues which stretch from each doorway right down the street. The shops have a habit of closing at some stage during the day and queues of patient, would-be shoppers wait in the cold.

Lorry-loads of melons arrive on the scene, or cabbages, and will be sold direct from the back of the lorry. In the area of the Consulate – not far from the Tauride Palace – you see the strange sight of massive drain-pipes running along above the pavements rather than beneath the ground. Maybe they haven't changed since the time of the revolution!

Here you see stone, Egyptian-type figures, two and three times larger than life, holding up doorways and windows. There is an air of decay. Though many of Leningrad's buildings are grand, most are in a sorry state of repair, with peeling paint, falling bits of masonry, broken drain-pipes. This applies as much to the recently-built blocks of flats; even their balconies don't seem to be straight! Houses made of wood on the roads out of the city lean in various directions.

Life's pleasures are simple. A queue forms around a hot bread stove, or a kiosk selling apples. You can have coffee and a cream cake for less than 40 kopecks. There are big advantages to the planned economy in terms of cheap travel and communication, even subsidised housing and cheap food when you can get it. But wages are low and the quality of life, never having reached a pinnacle, is now on the decline. Bureaucratic procedures in everyday life make for further aggravation. So many pieces of paper have to be filled in, taken to someone, stamped, taken somewhere else . . .

Even in the shops you queue – first to see the goods and find out the prices, then to pay and get a receipt, and then again to collect the goods! Most calculations in shops and canteens are still done on abacuses – rows of coloured wooden beads. Everything is weighed – even ice cream cornets sold from kiosks.

We saw something being sold like hot-cakes in the Metro station. A long queue had formed, and we thought there might be a new revolutionary newspaper at the end of it. A high-up officer in the army had joined the queue. We didn't know if there would be trouble but we joined the queue anyway. At last we got a copy of this much sought after newspaper and found it to be . . . 'Me and you'

– a dating magazine with articles about bio-rhythms and how to win friends and influence people!

The Leningrad Narodny Front

The Narodny Front sells a paper that costs 40 kopecks. One of the independent union journals costs one rouble for each copy to produce and sells for two roubles. It is illegal to sell this journal; it is illegal even to put a price on it! No doubt the thousands of people who acquire it make a donation, then get given it! We saw some opposition papers selling at three roubles, equivalent to nearly one-tenth of the wage of many workers! Such is the politicisation that, even at these prices, the material still goes like ice cream on a summer's afternoon, or perhaps in Leningrad on a winter's day!

During the course of the following few days, we discussed with a number of extremely serious people – some confused, some clear. Everyone is hyperactive. Discussions ranged from the current situation to historical questions, theoretical questions, international issues. 'What is your attitude to the ANC in South Africa?' 'What is your attitude to the NPA in Philippines?' asked the editor of *Rubikon*. This used to be the organ of the Campaign for the Democratising the Unions (CDU). Now it is linked to *Justice*, an independent Trade Union. This union is both an industrial and a political organisation orientated towards the Popular Front of Leningrad, which had a membership then of around 8000, including a large proportion of 'liberals'. He was satisfied with brief answers which summed up our opposition to both guerrillaism and opportunism. For Marxists, there is no substitute for winning the working class to mass action and the struggle for socialism.

He went on to explain he agreed with a lot of the democratic programme put forward by the Front. It is a rough programme and it is still not clear what they are going for, particularly on the economic questions. 'It would be worth having a look at the programme of this organisation and attending its conference at the weekend.'

The Leningrad Narodny Front is an umbrella organisation that brings together a number of currents who are against centralised bureaucratism and one-party rule. It started out as a group of people in favour of *Perestroika* – in fact as a 'pro-*Perestroika*' club. As in Soviet society as a whole, in the Leningrad Popular Front it seems as if **everyone knows what they are against but few know exactly they are for.** It is for reforming the electoral law and for fielding candidates in opposition to the Party monopoly, though many of its members hold Party cards. Members of the independent trade unions also participate. Its political programme is, however, ambiguous and unclear.

We were taken to meet two leaders of the Leningrad Narodny Front on the eve of their conference. They gave us an idea of what had happened at the time of the elections in March 1989:

'Early last year, the Baltics were already organising opposition. On 13 March 1988, Nina Andreyevna published her notorious letter in *Sovietskaya Rossiya*, opposing such movements. This we could not accept. We had a *Perestroika* club but we decided to set up an organisation *for* a Popular Front to strengthen the process of democratisation.

'We started a campaign called Election '89. There are 20 districts in Leningrad. There are 49 deputies, 20 elected through the districts and 29 through the social organisations. To give you an indication of what the election commissions do, in one case, we put forward nine names, but only one was allowed to go through. In the end, there were 35 on the Party list: all of them were thrown out. That included the First and Second Secretary of the Leningrad Party organisation and the First Secretary of the City Committee. Soloviev had to give way to Gidaspov, who became the First Secretary of the City Party.

'All six people that we supported in the second round got elected! When the result came through, it was like a big holiday – three days of holiday, of celebrating. Then we had to think what we had to do next!

'We agree on a number of basic things, like the elimination of the leading role of the Party. Our economic demands include multi-property relations, including private property. We want a decentralisation of the state economy, and factory collectives to control what happens. We should have maximum co-operation on the use of the social fund.

'We are for free trade unions, free press – an entire democratic programme. This should include the reform of the legal system, so that you have the right to a lawyer at the first stage of any trial.

'In the summer we had a rally 50,000 strong. Many of us support the Inter-regional Group of deputies: Yeltsin from Moscow; Ivanov from our city and Gdlyan, another Prosecutor who is taking on the *mafia*.

Together with *defitsit* – shortage – the word *mafia* seemed to be on the lips of the whole population, spat out with hatred. In some cases there are organised gangs of thugs and racketeers, who will not stop at violence to extort their gains. To most, *mafia* simply encompasses the whole bureaucracy. To Yeltsin, Ivanov and Gdlyan of the opposition deputies, it is the criminal layer

– the ones who have brought most shame to the ruling clique through amassing obscene fortunes. Yeltsin and his ilk must feel that their position is not secure as long as these scoundrels are bringing the whole system into disrepute. These criminals, along with the black marketeers, are an inevitable product of one-party military-police dictatorship. The Inter-Regional Deputies express the workers' indignation at the millions salted away by corrupt bureaucrats and they are themselves subject to various forms of retribution and persecution for their pains. This 'left wing' of the bureaucracy along with the 'centre' and the 'right' must fear that public rebellion against these hated elements could reach the scale of the Romanian revolution. They may now be assisting Gorbachev in a purge of the most corrupt elements of the bureaucracy, but this will not necessarily save them or prevent them being swept away in the flood of revolution which will develop sooner or later.

With the Leningrad Narodny Front leaders – obviously the sincere 'liberals' that Dmitri had referred to – we discussed Sweden, Britain, our programme and their programme. It became obvious that they had as yet unshakeable illusions in Yeltsin and Co. All their energies had been put into the struggle for democratic rights and no one had more than a hazy idea of how best to reorganise the economy.

This was to be confirmed at the congress itself, now taking place a day later because of difficulties with getting a meeting place.

The Conference

The Leningrad Popular Front conference seemed to be composed of predominantly middle aged people, quite a few academics and professionals and a smattering of workers, several of whom we had already met. People seem to belong to a number of different organisations, testing them out and shifting from one point of view to another. Many members of the Popular Front had started out as dissidents and moved into 'respectable' channels. Others had moved in a more revolutionary direction. A large number of Party members also participate in the Narodny Front, yet any speaker at the conference attacking the party was guaranteed immediate applause! One speaker urged the expropriation of the property of the Party – the papers and meeting halls and so on because they were supposed to be the 'property of the people'.

A woman spoke about the door-to-door canvassing her 'branch' was doing to build support for the Popular Front. Another speaker urged more effort to be put into the local 'self-management' committees. Someone speaking on housing decried the fact that you had to pay the same per square metre, regardless of the condition of the accommodation. In *Pravda*, we saw an item that gave the sanitary minimum for each inhabitant to be as little as 4.5 square metres. We have been told, however, that very many families live in less than this 'minimum'.

One of the aims of the Leningrad Popular Front is to ameliorate the conditions of the *Blockadniks*. Up to 200,000 survivors of the horrific wartime blockade have been living, as we had already heard, in 'temporary' communal housing; it has been temporary since the war! They have been told for decades that their future will be 'brighter', and just when there seemed to be a prospect of getting new housing, they have been told 'we need to bring skilled workers into Leningrad, and they must have priority. Tomorrow you will get your new home.' Even their pensions have been left behind compared with inflation and with the rising wages of those in work. '*Perestroika* has not brought results for these old people,' we are told by one of the founders of the *Perestroika* Clubs in Leningrad. 'They have been patient because they put up with wartime conditions for a very long time. They used to believe everything they were told; today, it has all been revealed to be false. Life for them does not make sense any more.'

The Narodny Front programme includes demands for the doctors and patients to decide who should go to which doctors and which hospitals. They demand an increase in investment into the health service of about 10 per cent; more information and statistics about health and the environment; more independence and control of the health and safety inspectorate; the breakdown of departmental barriers in medicine and an end to the vast differences between the facilities in the military hospitals and those attached to other workplaces.

The economic programme

Many of the Narodny Front's policies are for breaking down privilege and inequality. But the logic of some of these policies, as with those of Gorbachev and Yeltsin, will lead to new inequalities of wealth through wage and price reform and property ownership.

The economic demands of the Narodny Front include cutting the deficit and stopping inflation. But they also include the ideas of 'selling off' state industry, cutting subsidies, stopping the building of industrial plants and building creches and housing instead. This looks like allowing the cold wind of the 'market' to blow through the whole economy. Here again is the idea that the factories should be owned by their workforce and that land should be owned by the farmers. They based their case on the argument that 'in the USA, 10 million people owned enterprises'!

The idea gaining wide support in the USSR today, of self-management and self-financing as a counter to state monopoly, would lead to further dislocation and disintegration of the economy. Hostility to monopoly control and to the creaming off of funds by the central bureaucracy must be channelled in the direction of workers' control and management or end in a blind alley.

Technically, legally, the factories and the land in the USSR already belong to the whole population – they are publicly owned or owned by the state, supposedly being administered on behalf of the population as a whole. However, the mass of workers are alienated from any control or management of the use of the state resources, whereas the bureaucracy plunders the state coffers and the resources of every enterprise to reinforce its privileges. Many of the demands of active workers in the Soviet Union today represent, in a confused fashion, the searching for a better way to control and plan the resources of society. The people of the Leningrad Popular Front are searching desperately for some way of linking production to consumption, some way of overcoming the stagnation that now afflicts every pore of the planned economy. Public ownership and the plan were and still are priceless assets, but they have been mangled and enfeebled by the stranglehold of the bureaucracy so that we now see a state of disintegration.

The economists of the Popular Front see the fact that prices are not related to real productive value as a major stumbling block. Of course, in the context of chronically low productivity, allowing prices of commodities to reflect the amount of labour expended on their production would lead to massive inflation. The bureaucracy has stepped back on many occasions from 'freeing' prices to find their 'natural' level. They have feared a 'Polish situation' – the development of mass strikes and independent workers' organisations as a result. They have thus hesitated – only to find themselves faced with precisely such mass opposition!

These programmes of the various groups in the Narodny Front were pinned up around the entrance hall. They indicated how radical and far-reaching this democratic movement has become and also how beguiled many of the middle layers are by what they see as the success of capitalism.

One programme not adopted as the official programme of the Narodny Front, but put forward for discussion – included elaborate proposals for detailed changes in the law to allow the establishment of widespread share-holding. Shares were not to be the property of the few – after all, the movement is against all forms of monopolisation – but some way would be found of making sure that every worker had shares. It was hoped that this, coupled with control by the workers' collectives and 'self-financing', would perhaps unblock the clogged up wheels of the economy.

This one fact alone clearly shows to what a pass the planned economy and so-called socialism have arrived. 'Workers' democracy' has become a hackneyed phrase. All these developments are understandable, if the regime has claimed it is allowing control in the workplaces, through the workers' committees (STKs) and if the programme of Lenin and Trotsky has been suppressed and distorted over decades.

But the key to unlocking the planned economy is precisely the programme of workers' democracy. The factories, the offices, the means of production, and all the resources already belong to the working people. A lack of incentive stems from the knowledge that improvements in productivity and the results of extra effort would not benefit the population as a whole.

The point is not to replace a bureaucratic privileged, pampered caste with a class of owners of private property, but to fight for the regeneration of a system whereby workers and their direct representatives, including experts under their control, can make the decisions. With computers and modern technology, it is even more feasible than ever to ensure that production is geared to what people need and neither to profit nor to the interests of a bureaucracy. At present rigid targets bear little relation to the concept of harmonising production, distribution and exchange.

Undoubtedly, the Leningrad Popular Front was demanding more resources for construction and the introduction of new technology and a better distribution of the 'Social Funds'. They wanted an end to obligatory targets decided by the centre about what the enterprise should produce. They wanted more local independence and regional control of profits.

What kind of control?

In their eyes, conflict at present is not so much between the collective (workforce) and the administration (management), as between all against the ministry, which decides the price and what profit is taken. Without independence from the central state they felt it was impossible to have real 'self-management' – something that the government claims to be fostering.

A new law on the workers' collectives was introduced as part of *Perestroika*, and was supported by the Narodny Front, particularly those elements around the 'Democratic *Perestroika*' Associations. 'Formerly,' they told us, 'a quarter of the committee (STK) members were representatives of the management. Technically, what the committees decide is supposed to be implemented. At first the managements were afraid of these committees, but they have been reassured by the fact that, in practice, the attempts by work-forces to control what is happening has, as yet, yielded no concrete results.' These committees are anyway like islands in a sea of bureaucratic control – an opinion even held by members of the Narodny Front's sub-committee on self-management. Elsewhere, we were to find quite different results and different opinions.

The political programme of the Leningrad Popular Front is as much anti-monopoly as is its industrial programme. 'Marx was, after all, against monopolies' one member insists. They argue for 'de-monopolisation' by the Party of all areas of society. They are 'multi-party' and stand for all the basic freedoms including the right to representation at all levels. They aim to 'destroy the *nomenclatura* system'. 'The press, and means of information should be under Soviet control rather than Party control. The KGB should be under the control of the Soviets'. They stand for the 'direct election of the President, the right to hold referendums, for open debate at all levels and the right to know how each deputy has voted on every issue. Unveil the procedures on the distribution of housing, nurseries, jobs etc!'

It seems as if the people gathered in the Popular Front would be quite happy with a different way of running the planned economy, but no-one has yet come up with a coherent approach to this question. They seem to be searching for a market mechanism, some way of regulating the economy, of relating things to reality, of doing away with the distortions and subsidies and over-centralisation, but not at all considering the logic of what would happen if privatisation and cost-accounting were carried through to a conclusion.

'Now we have 6 million unemployed, even officially, and 1 million homeless at least', one of the 'self-management' activists admits. 'If they prune back on the economy the way that they say they are going to do that is going to mean 15 million redundancies, according to an economist on the television. Half a million tractors per annum are produced, compared with 100,000 in the USA, twice as much wheat, etc. What we have seems to be a 'prestige' economy, producing so many million tonnes of steel, but for the people in the street, they couldn't care less. They are not interested in running things.'

Little wonder! With long, tedious hours of work each day and after decades of having no influence, the initiative and the interest of the worker has been stunted. 'That's why the demand for the shorter working week is so important' we maintained. 'The Bolsheviks immediately cut the working day on coming to power. If workers were involved directly in the decisions that affected them, they would be able to eliminate waste and get increased wages. In this way, and on the basis still of a publicly owned, *planned* economy, it would be possible to develop a productivity level far higher even than that in the capitalist countries.'

We had to point out so many times that capitalists only produce what they think is going to make a profit and not what people need. We had continually to contrast the chaos and anarchy of capitalism with a planned approach to production. Whenever we described the horrific conditions in the West, nobody wanted to believe us! They have heard a lot of this before from their rulers, and regarded it as sheer propaganda . . . Nothing the bureaucracy puts forward is to be trusted.

Even the idea of a central plan – fundamental in providing the advantages of socialism as a system – has been temporarily discredited by association with a bureaucratic plan imposed from above. All the distortions and disruptions caused by the vain attempts of the bureaucracy to direct a giant economy from the centre without the involvement of the masses, has made state planning look unworkable. We from the West, had to be arguing the case for the plan as well as for state ownership. Some workers have illusions about capitalism and private ownership, but most firmly understood the benefits of the welfare provisions, security of employment, cheap housing and transport. Naturally, they want 'the best of both worlds'.

Capitalist restoration

The restoration of capitalism in the Soviet Union is not the most likely perspective. The press in the capitalist west is increasingly coming to the same conclusion. From their point of view, it is too expensive and risky, however much they wish to shore up Gorbachev's now shaky hold on power. This question, however, will be decided in the battles between the bureaucracy and the working class.

As the crisis in the economy deepens, different wings of the bureaucracy espouse different solutions. As Trotsky explains in *The Revolution Betrayed*, the starting point for the bureaucracy is their concern for power, prestige and income. In the initial period of the Soviet Union's development, imposing a plan from above, the bureaucracy was a *relative* fetter on production. As long as they could rely on a system which was taking society forward, they could count on at least passive support. Once they became an *absolute* fetter on the further development of society, everything was thrown into question.

Gorbachev's reforms have failed to solve the problems, and one wing of the bureaucracy wishes to call a halt. Gidaspov, the Leningrad party leader, started out as a Gorbachev man, and survived longer than other colleagues as he was not identified with the worst layers of the *nomenclatura*. Nevertheless, he has moved rapidly towards the camp of Ligachev, Andreyevna and co. who wish to put a stop not only to *Perestroika*, but to the movements for independence.

This wing will advocate force – the iron hand – even in relation to the Baltics. They will attempt to whip up Great Russian chauvinism which as yet gains little support in the major cities in the RSFSR. On the basis of events and the development of 'chaos', this could change. But a return to centralisation and Stalinist methods will not save the economy.

In the past, the economy of the Soviet Union grew faster than that of the capitalist world. Khrushchev boasted that the USSR would 'catch up and overtake the USA'. 'The present generation of Soviet citizens will live under full communism,' stated the 1961 Communist Party programme: 'The Soviet Union will reach the per capita production of the United States by the year 1980'.

The official figure for the growth of national production was three per cent in real terms for 1989. Even if this is the true figure, it has not lifted the Soviet economy out of crisis. It is also officially admitted that there are huge shortages, a budget deficit equal to 10 per cent of the national product, and 165 billion roubles of savings waiting to be spent on goods which are not available in the shops.

Meanwhile, although all the signs of a future recession are there, the world capitalist economy has continued to grow, widening the gap between the United States and the USSR.

In this context, one wing of the bureaucracy looks to a return to capitalism – the introduction of market mechanisms – as the only way to guarantee them their power, prestige and income. They say that *Perestroika* has been implemented too slowly. One group around the pro-restorationist Klyampkin, while admitting that 80 per cent of the population are against the imposition of capitalist relations, nevertheless say that they should be driven through by means of a coup. That would amount to a one sided civil war against the proletariat! Gorbachev and Ryzhkov stand in the middle – Prime Minister Ryzhkov advocates the privatisation of the economy to the extent of 35 per cent. Even this seems wildly unrealistic. All the capitalist commentators note a complete absence of the necessary profit motivation in Soviet society. There is no adequate infrastructure, and there seems to be an all-pervading consciousness that the simple ordinary person should rule, and that privilege and inequality should be eradicated, not fostered!

These sentiments are deep-rooted after generations brought up in the context of social ownership and a plan. The consciousness of the proletariat may have been thrown back, but not to square one. Not every trace of the principles and the programme which inspired the October Revolution has been eliminated. A strong collective spirit persists.

What unites all wings of the bureaucracy is their common fear of the spectre of the October Revolution which will return in the form of a mass movement of the proletariat to drive them from their positions. Fearless class fighters are already coming to the fore – in the factories, the shipyards, the mines and the offices.

The Narodny Front banner on the march!

Organising in the factories

THE DAY OF the Narodny Front conference, one of us went to meet Mikhail, an electrician at the Baltic shipyard.

'Four years ago I lost the sight in my right eye, so I was transferred to another job. The pay is 230 roubles a month, which means I get about 200 roubles after deductions. The work isn't hard but it's not very interesting. There's a lot of noise and dust so I think the wages should be higher.

'I pay two roubles a month subs to the shipbuilding union but I get practically nothing from them – no holidays or help with a holiday for my daughter. I live in a communal flat with one room, 13 metres square, for me, my wife and 17 year-old daughter – so there's nowhere for sex! There are five families in the flat, which has one bathroom, with hardly ever any hot water. In the morning you have to queue for the toilet.

'There's one telephone for which every family pays one and a half roubles a month. We all pay five roubles a month for the flat, one rouble for electricity and one rouble for the television. Services are cheap but the standard is very low. The chances of getting or buying a flat are practically nil.

'Last year, in our yard, we were supposed to go over to economic accounting, ie fixed profit distribution. The works paper published the profit distribution. The workers read it and put forward their demands to management. They refused to meet the demands and went back to the old system which allows them to decide pay arbitrarily.

'This year, after the miners' strike, we decided to set up a Strike Committee, which represents 39 shops and 10 departments. We've put our demands to management but haven't received an answer. The new law means they are supposed to reply in three days. Then it goes to an arbitration commission. Only then, if the dispute isn't solved, do workers have the right to stop work or call a strike.

'We expect an answer on 17 October. I've heard that management want to buy us off, but leave things as before!' Here the

discussion ended, but we would see Mikhail again with three other
workers and hear more of his story.

A strike in the Vyborg district

We spent the whole of one day with Volodya, a workers' leader we
had seen at two meetings already. He met us and took us on the bus
to his flat. He hadn't paid fares since they went up from 3 kopecks
to 5 kopecks and he argued anyway that Brezhnev said travel would
be free by now! (You can actually be fined three roubles for non-
payment of fare!) In the hallway of his flats was a notice announcing
the times when people could collect their ration coupons. He took it
down and gave it to us as a souvenir. 'Don't worry, everyone knows
the times'.

Volodya began by putting on a tape of his 'Songs of Wrangel's
Army' – lauding the White Army General's fight against Bolshevism – with the aim, no doubt, of shocking rather than entertaining
us. He succeeded! By the end of the day, however, he was keenly
discussing the ideas of Trotsky and the relevance of his programme
today.

Volodya lives and works in the famous Vyborg district of Leningrad. He has led strikes, he has participated in numerous illegal
protests. He showed us newspaper cuttings and photographs of
arrests during demonstrations, with the KGB hauling him down
from prominent places, statues etc.

Recently, when he had been put 'inside' for ten days, they had
shaved his head. 'They generally attempted to humiliate me because
of my so-called offences against the state. Then when I was let out I
was given an award, with a picture of Lenin on it, for being a good
worker – "a shock worker of communist labour".'

Volodya likened the STKs to the town and city Dumas – the tooth-
less councils set up under Tsarism. You could talk about what you
liked, as long as you had no effect on the decisions. In his workplace
they had called a strike through their own committee on 15 September last year.

'Under the economic reforms taking place at the moment, a new
system of wages has been introduced (Law 1115). Wage rates and
scales are supposed to be higher. For the bureaucracy – management – this has meant increased salaries: but for workers, at best it
has meant no change and in some cases a reduction in wages. There
are six scales, but when the rates were put up, people were put into
the lower scales.

'Workers have no protection because the so-called official unions have never defended the workers. Today inflation is beginning to rise uncontrollably, so workers' living standards are falling rapidly. On the one hand you have an objective cause for falling living standards – inflation; on the other, the subjective factor, the decisions of the bureaucracy. What I have described is generally the situation around the country. That is why the miners moved into action.'

At Volodya's works, management tried to reduce wages in the autumn of 1988. 'We have six sites to cover. We weren't prepared to accept what they were proposing and we began to prepare for action. At first we didn't propose a strike, but we went into negotiations with the management which lasted several months. A group or committee was formed. Four people played the main role. They had set up the STK, but, unlike the other factories, we didn't involve the management at all. We didn't get any support or understanding from the union, so we looked to other methods.

'We decided to organise a protest demonstration in front of the management's office. Permission to hold a mass meeting was refused because, they said, these matters could be discussed through "the collective" (the STK). Our district council and the executive of the Leningrad city were "hand in glove". In our society you have the trade unions, the civic organisations and the Party. And they are all tied up together. I went to a meeting of the party where I work, our pleading fell on deaf ears. That's why we had the idea of calling the strike. Articles 19 and 20 of the Charter of Workers' Rights 1954 guarantee the right to strike.

'On the twelfth we called a meeting of our collective – the nine leaders had all talked to the workers they represent. We declared a strike on our site for 15 September, giving management three days' warning. That was a decisive step. You have to remember that in Novocherkask in 1962, workers were shot. When we strike we strike against the state which has a very powerful machine. Any strike has a political significance.

'During the three days all was quiet. The chairman of the official union phoned up and said "What do you want – a Nagorno-Karabakh?"

'On the fifteenth all workers downed tools and came together in one place. A strike committee was set up. We understood we had to broaden the strike. We invited the TV and the press. They didn't write anything at first. The Leningrad evening paper only wrote about us months later and the reporter who did that has left the paper now! Two TV crews came – once during and once after the strike – but nothing was shown.

'We contacted the various committees we had been in touch with before. Fifteen minutes after the strike meeting the general director came to us. He started to threaten us: "You can either accept what we are offering or you can leave. If you don't want to work you will be dismissing yourselves." We replied that we were not out to damage production, but we were exercising the right to strike. The conversation went on for two or three hours in front of both workers and television cameras. In the end the director asked for a week to sort things out.

'We took a vote and the majority agreed, but, as we were leaving the meeting, we noticed the management had organised strike breakers – bus-loads of workers outside. So we immediately resumed our strike. The mood was varied. Some went into work at first, not sure which way things would go.

'The next day the Vyborg District Committee of the Party got involved to try and dampen things down because it was causing a stir with the radio and TV being there. Talks restarted. You had the management on the one side and the Strike Committee on the other. Either end you had the representatives of the Party and the official union. After a couple of hours, the management agreed in principle to all our demands but asked for time to work out how they could pay for them. We stayed out rather than go back on the basis of this promise.

'The strike lasted a week. Finally we had a complete victory. But this is not the end of it. On 20 July this year our STK drew up a new list of demands. We want improved material and technical supplies at the sites in order to be able to do the job properly, an immediate increase in evening and night pay of between 20 and 40 per cent with extra holidays and a reduction in the time we have to wait for housing.

'If these demands were not going to be implemented in full by 15 September, we reserved the right to take action. This was giving two months' notice. We had a mass of talks. The management conceded almost all our demands – eight out of nine points. The workers accepted that, but we gave them until March next year to implement everything.

'There are over a thousand in the workforce on 20 different sites. The management had to give all the other workers what we were demanding because they knew action would spread otherwise. I come out with 200 roubles a month. I pay the union 1 per cent and 10 per cent in income tax. If you have no children you pay more but no worker would pay more than 80 roubles a month tax.

'This flat was built 25 years ago by a co-operative. It's all paid for now but we pay 27 roubles a month for repair, common maintenance and services. Where people are still paying it is 60 roubles a month, compared with state flats which are around 20-30 roubles.

'Officially, we do a 41 hour week with standard shifts – a four-shift pattern – four nights, one day off and then mornings etc. We quite often do 12 hour shifts. We work amidst gas fumes, dirt, noise, coal-dust. We also work with asbestos and should be getting safer material. We should wear masks but they are difficult to work with. Our protective clothing is not very good and sometimes we don't get it. Sometimes we don't get soap. Supplies are getting worse. If you talk to people who were there 10 years ago they will say there always used to be plenty of towels etc, now it's different.

'In the winter, what coal there is will go to the big power stations, and the central heating depots will be the last in line. Three years ago when there was very severe weather – down to 30 or 40 degrees below – we wanted less gas to go to Finland but the authorities wouldn't agree.

'In reply to a question on the new trade union law, it is not a trade union law. It is a "law to resolve labour disputes" and we do come under that. But we will go through all the appropriate channels and, if we don't get what we want even when it goes to the Supreme Soviet, then we will look at organising a strike again. The law won't change anything.

'What happens depends on the economic situation. Where things are bad, people will strike. The miners' strike showed the government doesn't have any control. They can't stop us. They ban strikes and demonstrations in Nagorno-Karabakh, but they continue. They can threaten to dismiss us, but we don't regard that as too much of a problem. Management is scared. The secretary of the Party went round talking to workers on the shop floor. He saw the widespread anger at the current situation.

'What of the future? The general economic situation is so bad that it would take years to find a way out. Politically, in my opinion, we have an empire and what you see in all the republics like the Baltics is a struggle against the centre. You see popular fronts struggling for independence. Things could go two ways, either the Polish/Hungarian way or the Chinese way – Tiananmen Square. Something similar happened in Tbilisi.

'The KGB and NVD that were at work before, are all still there. You are in favour of workers' control, but we must have the possibility of putting that forward openly and freely. We must have a situation where people can come out without being killed. Then we can discuss questions of ownership and control.

'You say that you have heard that the KGB surveillance unit has been disbanded. Yeltsin says that these people are there for defence, but guns are being turned against the people and that must be stopped. We knew about Tbilisi the morning after it had happened through phone calls, but it also came across in the press and television. Already some people have been blamed and removed. One of our deputies in Leningrad told Gorbachev it was obvious who was responsible and everybody knows. Gorbachev said we would have to wait until after the commission reports for any action to be taken.'

Volodya told us: 'There are deputies who are saying that this is not a socialist country, but that Austria and Switzerland and Scandinavia are the examples to follow. The Democratic Union (of which Volodya is also a member) has a number of different factions, including "Democratic Centralists", "Democratic Communists", and there used to be "Christian Democrats" – but now they have set up their own organisation.'

There are certainly many cross-currents in the politics of the Soviet Union today!

We discussed with Volodya, as we had done with the students, and as we were to do with workers on many occasions, the 'programme of Terry Fields'. We pointed out that, of course, it had not been invented by him. It was was the programme towards which *Solidarity* in Poland had been moving in 1981. It was the programme of the political revolution in Hungary in 1956. It had formed the basis of Trotsky's struggle against the dictatorship of Stalin and the bureaucracy.

Lenin had formulated such a programme during the revolution of 1917, drawing on the experience of the first Petrograd workers' soviet in 1905. Even as far back as 1871, during the Paris Commune, such principles were being fought for.

This programme – for the regular election of all workers' representatives subject to immediate recall and receiving no more than the average skilled wage, for workers to run the state in rotation and even the demand for an armed people rather than a standing army – is the only basis for genuine workers' democracy. The right of all parties to stand in elections is a necessary element of this programme today. Volodya would think more about these points.

Our host for the day then took us to visit the notorious Peter and Paul Fortress. On our way, we went through part of the famous Vyborg district. As we passed one electronics factory with a workforce of 10,000, he mentioned that a 'strike committee' of 40 had been set up there, though as yet there had been no strike! Beside the factory was a huge hoarding with photographs of the latest 'heroes of labour' – town dignitaries soon to be completely exposed as empty men and women, a million miles removed from the courageous revolutionary fighters of this proletarian stronghold, who would tomorrow continue the proud traditions of the Vyborg workers of 1917.

The 'Vanguard of Labour' in the Vyborg

The middle layers

LATER THAT EVENING, two co-operators from Baku staying at our hotel wanted to talk to us. These computer experts told us that each ministry and government department now has computers, but they don't link up. They can't link up! They don't have the same type of computer or common programmes that allow for the exchange of information! These men also confirmed that the income of professionals has declined in the recent period. 'We don't know the figures, but we feel it in our pockets.'

Each of them received 150 roubles a month for the work they did in their department, but on top of that, they were making 500 roubles a month from their co-operative enterprise. They had invented a method of teaching languages through a programme which they wanted to sell to the world. These two men regarded themselves as budding capitalists, seeing 'private enterprise' as the only way to develop their invention.

We were persuaded by them to visit an exhibition of co-operatives. There was an array of talent and inventiveness crying out to be utilised. Ideas and inventions are stifled in the bureaucratic state system. 'We are capitalists', the computer experts joked. 'We only get half a per cent interest on money in the bank so we might as well use it to get a business going and develop our product.' People sharing a booth with them had devised plans and systems for measuring flows of various things, including gas, milk and so on. Other 'co-operators' had invented cranes for lifting vast sheets of metal in factories. Another had invented a very smart covered-in low-slung bicycle. At one stall was a notice in English touting the talents of a young man on offer for thousands of dollars.

A young woman we also met at our hotel was trained as a psychologist, educated, with a degree and so on. She had taken a second job as an interpreter, working with Intourist. She had just come back from Poland: 'People are smiling there' she said, 'It hasn't been like that for a long time. But it's feudalism here, you're tied to your job, you're tied to accommodation.'

She had been forced to work as a 'pedagogue' with old people, alcoholics, drug addicts. 'If you want to buy things,' she said, 'you have to have a second job.'

An explosion of frustration and anger is building up in every level of society. Educated people cannot tolerate the lack of choice in relation to jobs, housing, etc., *plus* censorship, *plus* the banning of books – it is an *indignity* that causes *indignation*! Before now, people had felt that eventually things would come right – now things are actually getting worse. Changes in psychology and people's consciousness are taking place. Many will fight, but many are lost in a fog!

Opinion polls – Russian style

We conducted our discussion with Yevgeny, a respected sociologist, seated round a long chess table in a room at the top of Yusupov House – a beautiful palace, now the headquarters of the Dramatic Artists.

'Three years ago, I was thrown out of the Institute for doing a survey at a theatre of what people thought about a play. Genuine social research had virtually disappeared. When there is only one candidate in an election, there is not much point in doing opinion polls!

'At the time of the March election, we went out onto the streets and asked who they would vote for. We interviewed two and a half thousand people and 75 per cent declared themselves for Yuri Baldirev, a 28 year old ship building engineer, as against the "Gauleiter" Anatoly Gerasimov. We had the figures ready a week or two before the elections, so we put the information to the Party Committee and publicised it, so that then if the result of the polls was 98 per cent in favour of Gerasimov, people would know there was something up – a "mistake".

'When they opened the boxes, 200,000 had voted and the result was just as we had predicted! We made predictions for 14 of the constituencies and we were within 3 to 5 per cent of the final result in all of them. It showed that although there was still pressure, people were not afraid as they had been in the past. Now we find there is very little resistance to the questions we ask.

'We also found out that people in the street are totally opposed to the "filter factor" – the weeding out of "unacceptable" candidates before the lists are finalised.

The National Question

'We have also seen a swing in the attitude of Leningradians towards the Baltic states. When the Baltics seemed to be doing unpleasant things to Russian people, the press was saying that they wanted to split. When we went into the streets, we didn't find any trace of an "imperial" outlook, or "Big Brother" outlook from the population of Russia, the largest republic. Fifty-six per cent said that if a majority wanted to leave the Soviet Union they should be allowed to do so. Thirty-one per cent said they should be stopped.

'In my opinion the Baltic question was not originally a national question. Socially they were well in advance, although now the national question has come to the surface but really what they are after is simply as much freedom as we have in our Russian cities.

'It's a different problem in Central Asia or the Caucasus. Frankly speaking, I don't know how we are going to get out of the situation in Nagorno-Karabakh. One year ago it was easier to sort out, maybe, but the inertia of the state now means that the situation is such that Ulster is nothing by comparison.

'Now the government is just desperately trying to keep the situation under control and stop the fire spreading to the rest of society. I have the feeling they think it is useful to keep that flame there as a pretext for moving in with the "iron fists".'

After the bloodshed in Ferghana (Uzbekistan) in the summer, the local Narodny Front-Berlik – invited Yevgeny and others from the Leningrad Popular Front to visit the area. 'They wanted us to tell people elsewhere what had happened and make it clear that it was not their fault. I went there with an ex-policeman who had been pushed out of the police force for his involvement in protests in Leningrad recently. From a distance we certainly didn't understand everything. The official version was not true and it didn't bear any relation to the facts.

'The first thing that struck us was the huge gap between the living standards in Leningrad and there. It would be as great as the difference between living standards in England and Leningrad. In Uzbekistan there are children who don't know what milk is. The level of exploitation of the peasants is greater even than was that of the negroes on the US plantations. Everything is polluted – the air, the soil – and this is having horrific genetic effects.

'All our society is corrupt but there is enormous corruption there. Power is maintained through knowledge of the Russian language. All others know Russian better than Uzbekhs. Cotton has always been the dominant crop, but, for Uzbekhs, the amount of land that they have is not sufficient for even subsistence production.

'The Meshketian Turks are super-proud Caucasians. There has always been some tension between the different nationalities but now when there seems to be no way out of the economic problems they have reached flash-point. It could have been any issue. It was quite by chance that the outburst was against the Meshketians; it could have been against any one of the other nationalities, for example the Crimean Tartars.

'The Russians are very frightened. They have lived all their lives in Uzbekistan and not learnt the language. They have been contemptuous of the Uzbeki culture and now they have to find a way of overcoming the immediate problems. They either have to go – and there is nowhere for them to go – or find a way of rapprochement.'

To our question on how history is taught in the schools, Yevgeny confirmed that history exams had been suspended. 'The textbooks were taken away and still have not been replaced. The courses have to be based on articles and digests.'

He told us that in September, there had been a Democratic Conference. Popular Fronts from 11 republics were represented, with people from a hundred different cities. The only ones missing had been the Azeris, the Turkmans, Kirgiz and Tajiks. Since our visit, explosions on the national question have had both a negative and a positive side. In some cases, they have been whipped up into bloody clashes. In others, they have shown the power of strikes and street demonstrations to remove corrupt leaders and to run society through popularly elected committees.

At the Scientific Institute

THE SOCIOLOGIST YEVGENY had told us that, on 23 August, there had been a demonstration against the Molotov-Ribbentrop pact. Up to 2,000 police had occupied the Palace Square. A hundred people had been arrested before the demonstration could even start. 'People had the feeling that it could have been another Tbilisi and they were frightened.'

When you live under an arbitrary, military-police dictatorship, there must always be that feeling that anything could happen. In spite of the massive power of the working class and the courageous and often unmolested activities of the opposition, the most brutal methods of Stalinist repression could be meted out, virtually without warning.

It was not without a slight flutter in the stomach, therefore, that we honoured our agreement to speak that evening at a public meeting in the Scientific Institute. We were told it was virtually a Defence establishment. Just to get into the building, names have to be given and passports shown.

The Institute has tens of thousands of students on different sites in Leningrad. It forms part of the famous Polytechnic – famous for the radical students that it housed in the period leading up to the Revolution. An interpreter had been booked and posters had been put up throughout the building.

The debate covered many of the issues we were confronting each day and helped clarify them in our minds. In addressing the members of 'This highly respected Institute', we expressed our views:

'The leaders of the capitalist nations are looking with delight at the difficulties into which the planned economies are getting. They are boasting that their system is triumphant on a world scale. In this, they are aided and abetted by labour leaders, who now claim that capitalism can be managed "humanely". Nevertheless, Marxists – scientific socialists – are convinced that capitalism has not found a way of avoiding crises and mass poverty. Even the present boom has fed itself on huge amounts of fictitious capital, and on a further impoverishment and super-exploitation of working people. Nine million live below the poverty line in Britain alone, three times as many as before Thatcher came to power.'

The implications of the bank rate increase (to 15 per cent), the effect on workers' mortgages etc., were unfamiliar concepts and difficult for the Russian audience to grasp. They could hardly believe the massive amounts of workers' wages consumed by housing costs and transport.

We pointed to the massive balance of payments crisis in Britain and America and to the panic on the world stock markets that had taken place that week. The bubble of the current boom in the west was bound to burst.

'Workers will move in their masses,' we continued, 'on the issues of wages. Like the mighty German working class, they will struggle for a shorter working week and against redundancies. The social democratic leaders of Europe are trampling underfoot the basic socialist programme on which the movement was founded.

'Many major unions in Britain, as well as the Labour Party, have in their constitutions the aim of establishing a society in which the means of production, distribution and exchange are publicly owned and democratically controlled. That clause – Clause 4 part 4 – of Labour's constitution had been inserted as a direct result of the inspiring victory of the Russian Revolution in 1917: now it has, in practice, been abandoned.

'These Labour leaders and the representatives of Capital have been helped in their ideological arguments by being able to point to the situation that exists in the USSR. When we argue for common ownership and socialism, our opponents say, "What, like you've got in Russia?" We say "No! Nationalisation of the monopolies? Yes! Plan of production? Yes! But with the full participation of workers in all the decisions about their lives, through representative bodies – at the workplace, at regional and national level. For all representatives to be elected and subject to recall and to receive no more than the average skilled wage".'

We explained about members of Parliament in Britain and that there were workers' MPs, living on a worker's wage. 'Terry Fields, for example, represents the "heroic city" of Liverpool – the "City that Dared to Fight". The Labour Council there conducted a momentous battle, mobilising the whole population of Liverpool. They gained huge concessions from the Tories, humiliating them and embarrassing the leaders of the Labour Party in the process. For their pains, the councillors of that city came under attack, not only from the courts, from the state, from the government of Thatcher, but also, shamefully, from Neil Kinnock and other right wing Labour leaders. The Marxist workers' representatives in Liverpool are enormously popular because they are prepared to fight to the end. They are prepared to put their jobs, their homes, their liberty, on the line in the battle against the enemies of labour.'

Rounding off our case, we claimed: 'The achievement of our programme would guarantee the survival of a workers' government and the development towards genuine socialism. Thatcher could try selling the *Daily Express* at the metro station (appreciative laughter), but who would want to turn the clock back? On the basis of a super-abundance of all the necessities of life and a shorter working week, at last art, science, technique and government would be freed from the control of a minority in society.'

The questions

Then the inevitable rapid-fire questions! 'What is your opinion of Sweden's socialism?' 'Are you for revolution?' 'What do you mean by working class, does that include self-employed and managers?' 'Will the revolution be bloody?' 'Doesn't it always lead to reaction?' 'What about the army?' 'Look at the French revolution!' 'Look at this country, 25 million unemployed!'

'Why did Lenin change his opinions and introduce "war communism" and the NEP if genuine socialism was his final aim?' 'In other countries, like France, haven't the workers come to power using humane methods of government other than dictatorship?' 'At least you have democracy in your country, our society is like Egyptian or Persian slave society.'

'Even unemployed people in Britain have cars. Here, even if you're working, it takes 15 years and a lot of money to get one!'

'Don't you think the crisis of capitalism is "objective" whereas the crisis of socialism is "subjective"?' 'Don't you have such things as collective enterprises?' 'Can you tell us where such things have been successful?'

One of the scientists seemed to think we were Utopian. 'Idealism was understandable at the beginning of the 20th century,' he taunted, 'but you must base yourself on the realities of today, not the dogmas of the last century. That's not real Marxism! You have to have a creative approach and choose between your "genuine socialism" and the socialism that we are building at present.' Disapproval of his comments ripples through the audience.

Another interrogator: 'Willy Brandt says that democratic socialism is not an aim but a process and that we can proceed with a mixed economy. Many fear a resurrection of private property that it would lead to an increased exploitation of man by man. Which do you think is preferable, a state monopoly or capitalism?'

'If increased wealth is a solution to the problems and capitalism is providing that, isn't collaboration better than confrontation or cataclysms?' 'Every government has to take unpopular measures.'

The answers

As usual, each point had to be answered as it came up and a chance to sum up was allowed at the end. 'But for the revolution,' we insisted, 'this country would still be on a par with India. In the '30s and again in the '70s, the planned economy had shown its vast superiority over capitalism. New life can be breathed into it only through workers' democracy.

'War Communism had been a valiant attempt to rebuild and develop a war torn economy. Lenin likened this situation of the new Soviet state, attacked on all sides by the twenty one armies of intervention, to life in a "besieged fortress" Hardships and rationing were inevitable. Some of the ideas put forward by the Bolsheviks themselves were simply utopian in the circumstances.

'Once the civil war was at an end, the peasantry who had reluctantly tolerated forced expropriations were no longer pre-pared to part with their products, if they were not going to be able to get the industrial goods they needed in return. Discontent was manifested in the Kronstadt uprising. The New Economic Policy introduced elements of the market into the buying and selling of grain, etc. Lenin had characterised it as a partial and temporary retreat. It could not be compared in any way to the wholesale attempts on the part of present-day economists like Abalkin to abandon socialism as an aim, and the planned economy in favour of a restoration of capitalism. This would represent not just a retreat, but a counter-revolution.

'After the working class takes power into its own hands of course it would still be necessary to utilise the expertise not only of scien-tists and technicians, but a layer of the managerial bureaucracy. Of course they would be entitled only to wages of superintendence and not the inflated income that most managers receive at the present time. Wages and salaries would at any rate be determined by the workers through their committees and all accounts be subject to their scrutiny.

'The revolution of October was not a bloody affair. As you prob-ably know, there were more deaths in the making of Eisenstein's great film *October* than in the taking of power itself. Only later, in

Moscow, were there some deaths – and even these were not inevitable. Counter-revolution is also not "inevitable", if the leaders of labour recognise the mighty power of the working class which has been demonstrated on so many occasions.

'When workers have power in their own hands, through committees that have developed, like the Soviets, as organs of struggle, then they will not squander opportunities and give breathing space to reaction. They can proceed then to use their combat organisations as councils for the most democratic and effective way of running society.

'The crisis of capitalism is rooted in the objective situation and a scientific, class analysis shows inevitably there will be further crises. Capitalists will stop investing. Here, the bureaucracy stops investing, or, rather, is at present cutting back on investing in capital goods in order to attempt to buy off the working class with an increase in consumer goods. This they are having difficulty achieving, and they will also find themselves with insufficient new plant and machinery to produce precisely these consumer goods!

'In Britain, we do have a so-called "democracy", but the right to organise in trade unions and to strike is harshly restricted. MPs are not subject to recall and they are far removed from the workers they represent. Thatcher and the Tories have been able to get away with banning *Spycatcher* for a time and have succeeded in the censorship of the press and television. This has not yet reached the same extent as under Stalinist regimes, but nevertheless society is ruled, not by Parliament, but by a tiny handful of monopoly capitalists and their "kept" representatives in government, in the courts and in the mass media.

'In France, the Socialist Party introduced reforms but they retreated in the face of a revolt by capital. Nor is Sweden a socialist country; it is dominated by a few big monopolies. It is totally dependent on trade with the capitalist world, particularly – in spite of its pacifist image – in arms. When the recession bites, the admittedly prosperous society of Sweden will be devastated. Already school students have moved into action to fight cuts in public spending, railway workers have been on strike, and car workers are becoming radicalised.

'It is true that nowhere do we have an ideal society, but here, in the USSR, it can be built!'

At the end of this very long meeting, a large man with brimmed hat and briefcase, assuring us that he was not a KGB man, asked us to convey his greetings to Neil Kinnock! As we walked out of the establishment, numerous other questions were fired – everyone was curious but everyone was friendly, too.

'A fortnight ago is history'

ONE DAY, WE snatched a quick look at the Smolny Institute, the headquarters of the October Revolution. It is still a Party headquarters and therefore visitors cannot simply wander around and poke their noses in the doors! We attached ourselves to a party of tourists and asked one of the stalwarts escorting us which room Trotsky had used. He answered in a completely unperturbed, matter-of-fact manner. 'He swapped with Lenin at a certain stage, so he ended up in the office you've just seen. His original room was just down the corridor. But it is not open to the public, like the rooms that Lenin used.'Nevertheless, this was certain progress.

Trotsky's photograph appeared on the wall of one of the rooms alongside other Bolshevik leaders. Not yet however, and not before the victory of the political revolution, will Trotsky be given his rightful place as a true co-equal and collaborator of Lenin. A recent poll showed 40 per cent to have a favourable attitude towards Trotsky without really knowing what he stood for. Another 20 per cent did not know. So nearly two thirds of the population is open to accept that Trotsky played an important role in the struggle for socialism and against Stalinism.

In Leningrad's 'Museum of the Revolution', there was a special exhibition on Stalin's crimes. It included a display of the vicious anti-Trotskyist posters he commissioned. One represents the great man who led the Red Army against 21 armies of intervention as a snake of counter-revolution! Another warns that Trotskyists are agents of fascism. A gruesome caricature of Trotsky depicts him as a monster to be throttled and another with half the face of Trotsky and half that of a criminal thug reads: 'Beware of men with two faces'.

Elsewhere, there were stunning posters from the early days of the revolution, brimming with audacity and confidence. There were designs for festooning Leningrad's squares and palaces with red to celebrate the first anniversary of the revolution. There were photographs, books and other mementos of the great class struggles of the pre-revolutionary period.

Amongst them were pictures of the workers of the famous Putilovsky arms factory, who played such a key role in 1905. There, too, were the formidable women workers of the textile industry who set off the February revolution in 1917. We saw the magnificent, still brightly coloured banners of the workers' organisations that had flown above many a revolutionary march surging over the bridges across Leningrad's canals.

Here also was a study used by Lenin after his return to Russia at the beginning of 1917. This building had belonged to Mathilda Kschessinska, a celebrated ballet dancer and mistress to Tsar Nicholas II. Her 'palace' had been 'confiscated' by the Bolsheviks, who promised to look after it. Following the 'July Days', the Bolsheviks were forced to go underground and the offices there were wrecked by government troops.

The study led out onto a balcony, where Lenin had declaimed to the crowd the ideas that were to be embodied in his *April Theses*. It was his decisive intervention at the Party conference which changed the direction the Party was taking and thus so dramatically changed the course of events in 1917. Lenin insisted that the struggle against the war, the struggle for food and for land must be tied up with the struggle for socialism – that there be no compromise with capitalism and landlordism! Lenin explained that, if the working class did not move to take control in society, no other class would find a solution to their problems. Millions more would be slaughtered in the trenches of the imperialist war and millions more would starve. Russia and its vast empire would be ground into the dust as a mere appendage and a colony of western capitalism.

If today, after crushing the resistance of the working class, capitalism were to return to the land of October, it would be purely as a predator. It would look on the Soviet Union merely as a source of cheap labour and fat profits. It would dictate terms that would reduce this great country to the conditions of the third world.

Life in the Soviet Union

On 20 October 1989, after a long trek and a long wait, we acquired an English language paper – the *New York Herald Tribune*. It was dated 13 October, so even this didn't give details of the crash in the stock market, merely a few of the warning signs.

On the same day, we saw a group of women huddled curiously round a table in one of the subways. On it were boots costing 150 roubles a pair and shoes at 65 roubles. That is a month's wages for the boots, and a month's pension for the shoes.

Many people seem worn out. Women, children, men on the buses and in the Metro are asleep, even literally 'out on their feet'. They have to spend hours and hours in the queues. We had seen one queue that went the length of a massive supermarket, down steps and along the pavement. We saw one queue for dried, flaked bananas. Long queues form outside the cafes, too. Even when you get your food, there is often nowhere to sit down! You stand up at the tables! No chairs – and also no knives.

You even have to queue to get into the filthy, insanitary public toilets! And, worst of all, you are charged 10 kopecks – twice what a journey right across the city costs. Some toilet charges are going up to 15 kopecks. The reason for this extortion is simple: toilets have been handed over to co-ops – they have been 'privatised'. Now the co-ops have the toilet monopoly!

Even state-owned canteens have been handed over to co-ops. The *Stalovayas* are relatively popular places offering cheap food at prices workers can afford. When they were taken over, either the prices doubled or the places were closed down. This is yet another reason for widespread hatred of the co-ops.

How will privatisation ever get a hold? Meat can be as much as six roubles a kilo. We saw scraggy cooked chickens in a co-op run street kiosk at nearly seven roubles. In the state shops, of course, meat may simply not be available!

We were told of one Leningrad family who have gone to America. The mother feels as if she is living in a seventh heaven. She has time to be with her children, instead of spending hours doing the washing, queuing at the shops, travelling in crowded trolley buses, etc.

The government currently has a campaign under the slogan 'A home for every family by the year 2000'. Some hope! There is a popular version of this slogan which goes: 'A home for every family by the year 2000 . . . in the graveyard!' There are signs of a massive effort to build more flats, yet many sites have stayed idle for quite long periods of time. Scaffolding and building methods look decidedly primitive.

We read that 1.5 million, out of the 5.5 million population of Leningrad, live in communal apartments where they have to share the bathroom and kitchen: 50% have no bath; 79% no hot water

Pyotr had mentioned to us in passing that because of his illness – asthma caused by the badly polluted Leningrad air – he cannot live in his tiny one-roomed flat with his wife and young daughter. He coughs through the night and would keep them awake. He stays with his mother; she sleeps in the kitchen so that he can have a decent bed.

Russian mothers are forced to care for their adult sons and daughters much longer than in other societies. Like most mothers, they are self-sacrificing and long suffering. But Pyotr tells us that his mother groans with complaints when Gorbachev's name is mentioned or when he comes on the television. 'Why?' 'Because there is nothing in the shops . . . People blame whoever is in power if there is nothing in the shops. There was a lot of support for Gorbachev in the first period but now it is rapidly disappearing. What is even more galling is that he is feted abroad as such a nice man. That angers people here.'

Only a few days before, we had seen Gorbachev on the television news being cheered in East Germany, where everyone, the item claimed, was celebrating the achievements of the economy in the spirit of *Glasnot* and *Perestroika*. Now . . . 'Honecker has fallen!' Pyotr tells us. He likens the appointment of Krenz to that of Gierek replacing Gomulka in Poland at the end of 1970. It is a measure which will prove incapable of stemming the tide of revolution. In the event, Krenz was destined for a much briefer appearance on the stage of history than Gierek!

Pyotr recounted an incident from the early days of *Glasnost*. 'It was impossible to hold large meetings openly. Once I went with 200 other people on a train for a meeting to be held in the open, in the countryside. None of us was allowed to know where we were to alight. Whispers would go up and down the train. Some get out at one place, some at another. Chaos and fear reigned and we ended up returning without the meeting ever getting itself together.

'You must appreciate how different things are now. Of course, you have been watched from the first day you arrived. You might as well accept you're operating in a greenhouse with glass walls! They will know about your meeting at the Science Institute, but so what? For the moment, they are unlikely to do anything. So much more is permitted now than before. You have to throw out your preconceived ideas and adjust.'

Discussion with workers

Life in the USSR can be grim – very grim. An appointment with a group of workers in an artist's studio takes us through dark, muddy yards surrounded by decaying, Dickensian tenement buildings. There are flies, small rats or cats, or all three in the corridors and stairways.

In the course of our discussion, the electricity goes off. It is not a power cut for the whole area, but it often happens in these blocks. The discussion, however, throws yet more light on what is happening to this country. The four workers we spoke with had come straight from their work on a Friday evening. They were members of the Leningrad Union of Workers' Committees, on which 12 plants were represented, in all 20,000 workers.

Yakov: 'The committees arise when struggles begin. Certain people come to the fore – they are not formally elected, but the workers support them. There is ample evidence of this every time so far. When we grow and establish real independent trade unions, no doubt we will have more formal methods. The STK (or Council of the Workers' Collective) in the factory are a sham.'

Grigori: 'In Yakov's bakery, he is known as the "Second Director" – everyone comes to him and he is seen as running things more than the real director.'

Yakov: 'Two months ago, we won a wage rise from 250 roubles a month to 350 roubles – a real increase! We demanded better pay and conditions and told management if they didn't agree, we would strike. In a bread plant that would cause big troubles, so high-up members of the Party committee came to the plant to discuss with me. The town committee is afraid of us making links with other plants. We gave them one month. Then they agreed and have fulfilled the agreement even though they can't afford to fund the rise. So, we have had successes, even though a lot of our workers are *limitchiks* – that is, their accommodation depends on their job.'

The *limitchiks* have come from outside Leningrad and live in dormitories in hostels. Three of these men had their own (cramped) apartments but one lives in a factory hostel – 'Not very pleasant', he says.

Yakov: 'Most of our work is done by hand – kneading and pulling and pushing, but we have a lot of accidents, with workers getting their fingers cut off – in the large mixing machines. Many are off sick for long periods with "industrial" complaints – bad lungs and particularly allergies. One of our main demands is for proper ventilation.

'Our shift pattern is four nights from 10.30 pm – 7.30 am, then one day free. Then, starting at 7.30 in the morning 'til 3.30 pm for four days, then one day free and four evenings: 3.30 pm – 11.30 pm. We were working all of these with no break, but one of the things we won was a break in the night shift.'

Mikhail: 'Last year in our shipyard, they tried to introduce night work without a break and without extra money. We refused. All workers in our country get 15 working days holiday – three weeks

– plus 3 other days. Management get 24 working days. The story that we can all go to holiday homes every year is a legend. About once every four years, we might get a holiday away paid for. For management, it's much more often.'

Grigori works at the Admiralty shipyard as a plater. There was a strike in the carpenters' department. 'It wasn't very well organised and was only against the immediate management of that department. Nevertheless, that management was completely replaced! And a commission of inquiry was established to look into things. After one month, it announced its findings. Predominantly management, the commission concluded that the department works badly because the workers work badly.

'It's still very hard working in there and many workers leave the department to go and work in the co-ops, where they can get two or three times the wages. Management tries to get workers to put up with the work by finding flats for them which ties them to the job. Management is proposing elections for the head of department as a sop.'

Mikhail: 'In the Baltic shipyard, a strike is due in one department. Our demands have been put forward for more pay and better conditions and we are preparing to get other departments involved. We have now given management until December (when all the collective agreements have to be signed) to come up with what we want. They have said the pay will stay the same, but the conditions would be improved.

'We work on the big tanks (containers) for cooking food. Each one is sold for 55 roubles. Admin says that's too high and they put the price down – at the expense of the workers. We are supposed to be changing from military to civil production – consumer goods – boiling pans for domestic use, plastic things, furniture, locks, chess sets. It will mean lower wages, we know.

'Grigori's plant is going over to agricultural equipment. The technology is being prepared, but management are not really interested. They got more money for defence work also . . . they're quite happy with their nice flats, cars, dachas, etc.

'We work with some machines that are 100 years old, others date from 1903! We know changes need to be made, but we are the ones who know how to make them. We use a special kind of steel that is uncomfortable to use and a danger to health. We have a network of activists in the factory which has 39 shops and ten departments. Because we produced military ships, the Department of Security kept a very tight control but things are changing.'

Grigori: 'You could only go into the yards with permits before. If we challenge anything, we come under pressure. They can move us to another department. They try to play one yard off against another. The authorities play on fear, but if it comes to a strike we will 'phone up other factories to help.

'We are demanding genuine elections for the trade unions with ballot boxes at the front gates of the workplaces. At the moment, we vote for "electors" who quite often don't vote the way we want them to for the committees. We want direct elections.'

Ilya: 'We want as much contact with workers in other countries as possible. *These days, anything that happened a fortnight ago is history.* We have been considering how to make use of the official twinning of our cities with cities like Dublin, Cardiff, Manchester, but only official links are allowed. Unofficial links are more difficult.

'We are bringing out 2,000 copies of our own paper, but need a lot more and need printing equipment etc. We want exchange of experiences and material on organising at work, agitation, strikes, and visits. When we had our strike a month ago, we didn't have access to printing equipment for producing leaflets.'

Grigori: 'Gorbachev visited the shipyards. He only talked to management and they had the place decorated out especially for the occasion. The words *Glasnost* and *Perestroika* have lost any meaning now. The plan is supposed to have been fulfilled but where are the results? Prices are rocketing.'

Ilya is a hod carrier and speaks fluent English: 'Our construction workers' strike a month ago was on TV. We wanted more wages. (In co-ops 40 per cent of every rouble made goes to workers – in state industry 17 per cent). We wanted our pay to reflect the work we do. There are six deaths per 1000 workers in our industry. We have nowhere to change our clothes and cannot get clean because of the shortage of soap. We wanted our foreman sacked. Management agreed to half our demands but said they didn't have enough money for the rest. We started our strike and they found the money!'

This may be our last day in Leningrad. We have to go to Moscow and may not get back. As we travel through the town for one more discussion, we note how old-fashioned all the vehicles seem to be, as well as how covered in dust and dirt. It is as if nothing has changed since the 1930s or perhaps 1950s at the latest.

Pyotr, our guide and mentor for much of our time in Leningrad, is fluent in foreign languages without ever having the chance to set foot outside his country. How had he mastered so many? 'It's a strange story. I learnt some in my school days, of course. But, you see, each enterprise has to provide labour on the collective farm that is linked to it. I was always volunteering to do extra duty at harvest time because I found myself with hours to spare between each load that had to be checked. I used those hours to read and to teach myself languages. You'd get your normal pay – and extra – and time to read! What more could you want?'

We discussed as far as the station. There we make a phone call to one of the local trade union leaders, who tells us that independent trade unions are now being established in Bulgaria. He is very excited, but Pyotr is sceptical. He thinks it is possible that they have called a press conference and announced their existence, while having no real substance. We'll see. By the beginning of 1990, *Podkrepa*, the Bulgarian independent union, had already become a force to be reckoned with. The resurgent forces of the working class are on the move throughout the Stalinist world!

In Moscow

BY COMPARISON WITH Leningrad, Moscow is a much vaster city. It has fewer ancient buildings. Those that have survived war and conflagrations are beautiful, but many of the churches and cathedrals are dwarfed by ugly grey state hotels, with thousands of rooms. Most buildings are massive, some of them monstrosities. The statues, the parks, the gateways all seem to have been designed to be bigger and better than anything else that could be found in the world – 'concrete proof' of the superiority of Stalinism!

With nine million people, Moscow is the second largest city in Europe. Most inhabit gigantic tower blocks on the outskirts, which loom one after the other as far as the eye can see. They stand in bleak, muddy wastelands, often bordered by noisy, fume-ridden motorways. The Moscow working class trudges along dimly lit pathways made impassable with puddles the size of ponds. Every tube, tram and trolley bus is packed and, in the vast workers' suburbs, they seem to arrive far less frequently. Long waits in the biting winds or gusty rain are just part of life.

The population of Moscow seems much more cosmopolitan, much more mixed, than that of Leningrad. There are more Asians and Turks and Africans. There are also more people begging and more people moving about in the subways with large cloth bundles or cardboard boxes. One man on the metro has a bag full of tins of chicken – between 15 and 20 of them. Can this be hoarding, or is he going to have a big party?

While we are there, we see an extraordinary Sunday night television programme which has people throughout the USSR glued to their sets. All kinds of people – disabled or inadequate, young, old, fat or even wasting away – are called to the microphone. They explain the most personal of details of their life before an audience of millions. A girl struggling to walk, a man with a classical drooping moustache, a peasant woman, each took their turn.

The compere Kashpirovsky seems to be getting people to air their problems, reassuring them and possibly even laying claim to be some kind of miracle healer. This programme, with a strong element of the mystical about it, is widely considered, we discover, to be part of quite a deliberate school of mystification. There has been a resurgence of articles in the press about flying saucers and extra-terrestrial visitors.

Moscow News comments that, in the early years of *Perestroika*, all such programmes and letters to the papers disappeared. Life itself had held promise and was too interesting for people to want to escape. Now, with its accumulating problems, the regime finds it useful to develop a mesmeric fascination with the supernatural once more. On our return, we learnt that Kashpirovsky's programme has now been taken off the air.

We visit the famous Arbat, where we find illegal paper sellers and portrait artists plying their trade. A discussion starts up between us and the paper sellers and lasts more than two hours in a stand up open-air cafe. They are heavily involved in a campaign against the vicious internal passport system. Workers are prevented from moving out of one city to another, if it doesn't suit the regime. Even pensioners are not allowed to move to where their families have settled. One of these lads, Oleg, is squatting and has no fixed address so that he can carry on his work of selling an illegal paper and organising an illegal campaign with less risk of getting tracked down.

A coffee drinker at another table joins in the discussion. 'How can *I* buy shares? How can *I* get another job? People are leaving their jobs to go into co-ops to get better money.' 'With the extra prices they then charge,' we add, 'this process can only be at the expense of the working class, and cannot be a lasting situation.'

This woman agrees, complaining that 'it costs 70 roubles to buy the cheapest of jackets; 140-270 roubles for a decent one and 800-1000 roubles for a good coat. Even then, the quality is not up to that of Western standards.' Nothing has changed since 1936 when Leon Trotsky explained that 'Quality escapes the bureaucracy like a shadow'.

'Forty per cent of the population is said to live below the poverty line (70 roubles income a month). The average wage is 200 roubles', Misha, one of the young men at our table explains. 'But I need at least 250 roubles to maintain my wife and young child with food and other necessities.'

'Pears, for example,' the woman continues, 'have gone from 7 kopecks to two roubles.' Like so many we have met, she could see exactly what was wrong, but wasn't at all clear on a solution. But she was keen to express herself. 'Ninety five per cent of what is produced, **they** decide what is done with it – the *mafia*. The factories produce because of what the bureaucracy says, not because of what people need.'

Education is not good enough either, insists Misha. 'Too much time is spent on propaganda – so-called Marxist theory and analysis. This is no help in training you to be a biologist, for example.' We would favour genuine political discussion on *all* academic courses, but not the dry and sterile diet forced down the throats of today's generation of students.

We were questioned closely on life in Britain. Then, once more Sweden was held up as a model. Once more the October revolution was labelled an 'overthrow'. Once more also Lenin is blamed for starting the Stalinist repression with the banning of political parties. Forced collectivisation had been a crime, they said, but Bukharin had been right on the question of the peasantry.

Perhaps this is simply echoing the current official line, but Trotsky pointed out how wrong the current policy was. Bukharin's appeal to the Kulaks – the peasants with the largest landholdings – to 'enrich yourselves' was a recipe for counter-revolution. Forced collectivisation had been a violation of Lenin's approach. The technological means for rapidly developing agriculture were not yet to hand and collectivisation should have been entirely on a voluntary basis. Proceeding by convincing peasants of the benefits, it would inevitably have been a slow and gradual process.

The banning of parties and factions in the early days of the revolution is now being falsely given as a reason for the existence of the one-party dictatorship in the Soviet Union. Lenin and Trotsky felt both were a *temporary* necessity when the young workers' state was under the threat of being overthrown. An attempt had even been made on Lenin's life. They intended that these bans should be lifted once the danger to the state had passed. Today, there can be no justification for the banning of parties and of factions inside the ruling party.

In Moscow, we met many people already decked out in three-piece suits, ready to enter the Congress of Deputies on the backs of the masses' desire to be rid of the old one-party state. A number of apparently well-meaning 'liberals' were already there. They had been thrown forward in the first undiscriminating wave of the democratic upsurge and were regarded as people's heroes. Amongst them were Yeltsin, Ivanov, Gdlyan and (at that time) Sakharov too. They have come under attack from the right and even sometimes from Gorbachev. These prosecutors and deputies, still (at the time of writing) loyal members of the Party bureaucracy, have taken up some of the workers' problems and have taken on the enemies of the workers – notably the corrupt gangster elements of the old elite.

The mood in the 'Red Belt'

The popularity of some members of the liberal wing of the bureaucracy could not have been more graphically demonstrated for us than by a meeting at which a number of them were due to appear. Thousands congregated at the civic centre in the sealed city of Zelinograd. Unaware that no foreigners were supposed to travel to this part of the 'Red Belt' around Moscow and also unaware even of our destination, we had been bundled into a taxi by two of our friends and sped with them through a dark and stormy night. We found ourselves in what must be one of the most militant hot-beds of the democratic phase of the revolution.

Outside the meeting hall, as the crowds gathered, placards abounded: 'Expose the *mafia* and return the millions to the people'. 'United Front of Workers' Collectives – children of the reactionary Party apparatus.' 'We demand an end to the provocations against our deputies – Yeltsin, Gdlyan, and Ivanov!' 'Hands off Yeltsin'. Even 'We approve Yeltsin's trip to the USA'. 'Yeltsin, Gdlyan, Ivanov – the people are with you'. 'Down with the slanderers'. 'Comrades of Zelinograd – defend our deputies from attempts to discredit them'. People were proudly sporting lapel badges with Yeltsin's portrait on.

Within minutes of our arrival in Zelinograd, one of our travelling companions was arrested for selling his paper. 'He'll only be held a few hours!' said his comrade.

Before the doors were opened, we had been taken under the wing of some of the largest proletarians in the throng. At the sound of shattering plate glass, our 'protectors' told us instinctively that this must simply be a provocation on the part of the Party – nothing to do with the people genuinely trying to get into the meeting. Inside, we were treated like royalty. Front-row seats were cleared of their occupants – for 'the English'! We protested with embarrassment but had to acquiesce.

The meeting had been organised by the 'Zelinograd Society for Democratic Elections'. A number of similar organisations of 'electors' exist throughout the workers' suburbs of Moscow. Many of the organisers (and the speakers) were long-serving members of the Communist Party, yet they had had a battle even to get the premises to hold the meeting. The Secretary of the local party had tried to block it. This news was greeted with whistles and boos at the beginning of the meeting. 'It is not the anger of the town committee that we have to fear, but the wrath of the people,' (Loud, enthusiastic applause!) At a suggestion from the floor, the whole hall stood in protest at the Party.

One or two questions were asked, then the whole meeting waited while a wrangle took place with the hall management to get the proceedings of the meeting relayed, not only to the overflow hall, where hundreds more were packed in, but to the many more hundreds waiting outside the building in the pouring rain! More than two thousand must have crammed in to the main hall with a seating capacity for 1200.

The meeting waits

The atmosphere was electric and euphoric – reminiscent of the scenes in the Smolny described in John Reed's great account *Ten Days that Shook the World*. Here, people were neatly dressed, not coming in straight from the battle front. The demands were still modest – not for the taking of power, but for the right to elect representatives freely and without dictatorship from the Party. The placards declared, 'We are for equal, secret, direct elections of the People's Deputies'. 'Against district pre-election assemblies.' 'Against elections from social organisations.' 'Down with the plant electoral circles.'

If this is the first phase of the revolution – the spring – what is the next phase going to be like? We only hope we will have the privilege to be there when it happens!

That may not be long. Already loyalties have shifted fast, not only from some of the hated figures like Andreyevna, Saleyev and Smirnov, and from Gorbachev. But one speaker at this meeting even denounced 'that so-called "dissident", Medvedev'. He had tried to water down a commission inquiring into the guilt of the gangster Smirnov by making it just a 'discussion'. They were also angry about attempts to prosecute Gdlyan and Ivanov for trying to pursue Ligachev into court on charges of corruption.

This issue came to the surface again in the New Year, by which time some people were commenting that Gdlyan and Ivanov's credibility was wearing a little thin, as they had still produced no evidence in spite of promising it since the summer. Uncritical support will not last for ever, when the results do not materialise.

The packed meeting in Zelinograd

The Zelinograd women's picket

The meeting begins

In the highly charged atmosphere of this Zelinograd meeting, as soon as it was announced that at last the people outside could hear the proceedings, a deafening cheer went up. Speaker after speaker demanded 'an end to the monopoly of the Party' – 'Down with the leading role', etc. Apologies were given for Yeltsin, Gdlyan and Ivanov, who all happened to be either ill or abroad. Obvious disappointment was quickly dissolved by excitement as the meeting got under way.

A woman standing-in as a speaker for Yeltsin declared: 'There is no need for hero-worship, but Yeltsin has spoken out against the apparatus, in favour of *Perestroika*. He is leading the political struggle against the way things have been done for so long . . . There is a hunger in the country for knowledge – to know what is happening . . . We must have a battle of ideas and fight for our programme . . . Why are our enemies slinging mud? Because they resist our demands.'

An investigator from Gdlyan's office asks: 'Which direction are we going in? Which forces are going to win? The deputies have been told they cannot put a resolution in support of Yeltsin because this would be divisive. This is what we get from people who are constantly trying to divide workers – against each other, against the intellectuals, etc. And people like Medvedev are trying to protect the *mafia*.

'The Partocracy is a Plutocracy. If the *mafia* is operating, the people at the top know about it. Medvedev said "no commission", but Smirnov's guilty!' (Cheers from the audience.) 'Until this plutocracy has been got rid of, nothing will change in this country!' Enthusiastic applause and shouts of approval.

A correspondent from *Argumenti y Facti* – renowned for taking on Gorbachev – received a tremendous response from the crowd with his demand for a totally free press. A local man took the mike: 'We want representatives who think of themselves last, not like the people we have at present. Our representatives should be conducting an all-out struggle against the worsening food situation.' A doctor stepped forward to speak about the dangers, not only of the people's inadequate diet, but even the dangers within the food that is available – the chemical adulteration, carcinogenic substances etc.

People's Colonel

A retired or 'reserve' Colonel, in full uniform, bursts onto the stage waving a clenched fist in the air. 'The KGB is . . . a fascist organisation!' he declares to screams of delight – and this despite the fact that the KGB have recently been trying to appear far more user-friendly! They have held 'phone-in programmes, and made promises to dissolve their worst units. The Colonel thunders out 'I am a Colonel of the People! While these people at the top hold a gun to our heads, we cannot feel at ease. Ligachev and Company have sold our wealth abroad, so they could fill their own bank accounts in Switzerland.

'The army will not use arms against the people. They tried to get rid of me three times. Next year's elections have to be a tremendous threat to the bureaucracy – the people could take power off them. Long live the people!' (Tumultuous applause!)

An enthusiastic collection was taken to help finance the campaign. Advice was given on what to do if arrested on the demonstration planned for Red Square the following day. Votes were taken on a number of resolutions, including one to organise a separate contingent on the 7 November march to commemorate the anniversary of the October revolution.

A motion of support was to be sent to the commission looking into the Yeltsin-*Repubblica* affair.

A special appeal was made to the meeting for all workers to work Saturdays to get money to produce a paper for the movement. An announcement was made of the demonstration that was to be held around the Lubyanka prison – the KGB headquarters – on 30 October, 'International Political Prisoners Day'.

Yet more speakers denounced 'the Congress of Puppets' and spoke of 'our revolution'. A declaration that Afghan war veterans supported the movement nearly brought the house down. A woman from Armenia, who had been in Moscow for three months, made a poignant plea for help. She had lost three sons. She had been imprisoned twice.

'The only road is with the workers!'

A student shouted from the platform 'The only road is with the workers . . . **but how can we proceed**?' Another orator burned with indignation: 'Gdlyan has been denounced as a "future Beria" and Yeltsin likewise.' He hurled juicy accusations back at the country's leaders: 'The Central Committee are more than half-drunk most of the time.'

Then calm was called for as an amateur video of a recent protest was shown at the end of the meeting. The Zelinograd people had formed a human chain from their town to the centre of Moscow on

7 October. The film whirred on amid great laughing and rejoicing of the assembled crowd. This was almost the end. Just as you thought the meeting was finishing, it would start up again! No one wanted to go home, they were enjoying themselves so much!

Conclusions? It seems as if Gorbachev is now completely discredited. Even so, the hatred of Ligachev and his supporters and the terror of black reaction – of a return to the horrors of the past – could possibly still save Gorbachev, if he came under attack.You only have to see the strength of hostility to reaction in votes in Spain and Greece. The so-called socialists there had for long failed dismally to satisfy the needs of the workers they claim to represent, yet workers continually voted **against** the right. Surely that colonel and the investigator could not have done anything like what they did tonight this time last year.

It is obvious that even these 'militants' are unsure of how to proceed. They know what democratic rights should be theirs, and that nothing should be allowed to stand in their way. But they are uneasy about the future. One of those who had escorted us into the hall – an engineering worker – had spoken of 'a big moment for Russia', but added 'People are afraid that the present situation will not last long.'

There are 170,000 workers in this town and they are clearly already developing a revolutionary reputation. They cheer their leaders to the echo – the representatives of Zelinograd and Moscow. But even these 'heroes' are riding a tiger. Many of them will not pursue the workers' cause 'to the end'. That task will fall to the **real** Bolsheviks of the future.

What kind of democracy?

In the future, real Soviets, councils of workers delegates, will come into their own as organs of struggle and organs of workers democratic rule. But so discredited have the existing Soviets become, and to such an extent has the Communist Party abused the principle of giving predominance to workers in government, with the system of reserved seats, and of elections through the workplaces, that they are now hated.

Genuine Marxists support the demand for territorial elections and the direct election of the President. Such elections are seen as an enormous step forward by workers who have been denied every kind of democratic expression for 60 years, but of course, they would not in themselves put the running of society into the hands of the workers. Supporting steps towards democratisation,

Marxists also support the organisation of independent committees of workers in order to pursue their interests and formulate their own socialist demands. Even workers' councils – soviets – will be necessary once more, both as organs of struggle and as the most democratic form of workers' rule.

In the forthcoming elections, the key issue for gaining mass support is a programme that links the immediate problems facing workers, and the need to purge society of the bureaucratic caste, which stunts its further development. Such a programme would include an immediate cut in the working week to 40 hours and then to 35 hours. A minimum wage – probably of around 400 roubles a month. A crash building programme for decent housing, schools, hospitals. An end to all privileges, no sale of state assets, and for a democratic plan of production, through workers' control and management.

The Zelinograd meeting

Moscow life

WE WERE BROUGHT down to earth with a bump. On the way back to the centre of Moscow the night of the Zelinograd meeting, we saw a man on the Metro covered in blood – around his face, neck and hands. He didn't look drunk, just badly beaten up. We were reminded of the brutality of society. On a previous day, we had witnessed a fight of youth in the street. One of them had had his head repeatedly kicked. We had seen many people – men and women – the worse for drink and drugs. This was confirmation of reports we had seen of the rapid degeneration of society and an escalating crime rate.

We had occasion to reflect on how little the safety of ordinary people counts for. We saw a car that had been involved in an accident, driving around freely in the city with jagged pieces of metal and glass sticking out at the front. This would be illegal in Britain as both children and adults could be badly injured in any brush with such a vehicle. In the USSR, there are few such laws on safety, and even less enforcement.

Yet, by contrast, for the protection of the bureaucracy, no expense is spared. Vast forces of the state exist. We noted both in Leningrad and the capital city, Moscow, large numbers of uniformed officers – many with briefcases attending the numerous academies; many simply keeping a close eye on society. You are no doubt meant to feel that the state is omnipresent. It is noticeable that ordinary soldiers in uniform mingle a great deal with the local population. This is a double-edged sword. These soldiers, especially the large numbers of conscripts, will inevitably be susceptible to the pressures of a mass movement against the powers-that-be.

The Red Square demonstration

The planned demonstration in Red Square to lobby the RSFSR Supreme Soviet is obviously not going to take place in the square

79

itself. The vast area outside the Kremlin walls, between St Basil's, the GUM Department Store and the Historical Museum is blocked off by crowd barriers and rows of policemen. We ask, as good tourists with our cameras, why we cannot enter Red Square. 'There are people who do not want the Supreme Soviet to do its work.' we are told.

We find some of the Zelinograd women picketing the massive Rossiya Hotel, with their placards. They are armed with carnations and individual letters to give to each deputy when they arrive as expected for their lunch. They intend to let the deputies know, in no uncertain terms, what they want them to vote for. One of the placards is a quote from Stalin: 'It matters not who votes, or how they vote. It matters who counts the votes.'

We talk to one of their leaders – the woman from Yeltsin's office who spoke at the meeting the night before. She is very articulate about the demands of the movement, but, on the longer term aims, she is forced to admit, 'No one is clear on the question of ownership. Perhaps a free market would be an improvement, perhaps it would be worse? Who knows?'. She talks to us undeterred by the rough handling of some of the police.

Another unofficial meeting has formed at the other end of Red Square – on the pavement beside the Lenin Library. A group calling itself the 'Association of Electors of the Red Guard District' have a megaphone. A young man with a beard and scarf and Lenin cap speaks through it earnestly to a crowd hidden under a sea of umbrellas!

Placards declare: 'No to the sixth article of the constitution' – this is the one that guarantees the 'leading role' of the Communist Party; 'Self-renovation of the Soviets'; 'We are for direct elections on a territorial basis'; 'Is it only the people who are hungry and the Partocracy which is fed?'

Ordinary life

That evening, we are invited to the home of one of the Arbat paper sellers for a birthday meal. We will discuss their campaign, but it is also his birthday and there will be goose as a special treat! This is a chance to find out much more about the day to day life of the Russian people. Not all rents are pepper-corn. This couple pay 150 roubles per month for their flat. Misha is a laboratory worker with a wage of 200 roubles a month. Inevitably, he does a second job.

For a phone in your home, you pay 2.50 roubles per month, and

'It matters not who votes.....'

The Lenin Library demonstration

all your local calls are free – but it costs 100 roubles to get the telephone installed. Even if you are on decent wages, consumer durables are often out of reach. You might have to work 15 years before your turn comes to get a ticket from your work place to be able to buy even the smallest of fridges, which could cost you between 160-180 roubles. A bigger fridge would be anything from 500-700 roubles. An automatic washing machine would be 300 roubles, but again you have to wait until your number comes up, even to be considered as a purchaser. Then you have to find the money. A cooker could be anything from 130 roubles – much more for an imported one.

A car on the 'white market', if you are lucky enough to get to the end of the queue for one – after 5, 10 or even as long as 15 years – comes in the region of 16,000 roubles. On the 'black market', you might be asked for anything up to 32,000.

'Shopping for children's clothes is a nightmare,' says Misha's wife, Ana. 'A child's shirt can cost as much as five roubles; a suit between 20-25; a coat 20-30. Shoes are worse. Often you can't find any at all.'

Ana is 19 and has a child of 18 months. All.three sleep in the living room with a double bed and a chair-bed for the child. It is the only room in the flat, apart from a small kitchen and miniature bathroom with peeling walls. Their curtains are transparently thin. They have a tiny black and white television, few ornaments, very few books and, as far as we could see, almost no toys at all for their bouncy, inquisitive child.

Ana is constantly changing woollen tights on her son – at least four times that we noticed in two hours. 'Washing the old fashioned kind of nappies is obviously difficult with no machine. Can you not get disposable ones?' 'You must be joking! What chance have we got of getting disposable nappies if we can't even get toilet paper!'

'In the queues,' Ana tells us, 'the old people say "Things are not as bad as they were during and after the war".' What do they think of Gorbachev? 'They used to say he speaks very well, not like Brezhnev,' (and she mimics him pathetically smacking his lips). 'Now they just swear and grumble.'

'What are people thinking of when they are in a queue?' 'Very little, really, just what, if anything, is going to be available when they get to the counter! People will buy 20 packets of anything if they think its going to run out.

'The highest pension is 130 roubles; for ordinary people, it is around 95 roubles, but some can be as low as 30 or around 70. The co-ops are not liked by old people. Rationing actually started in 1980 with salami. Then in 1986-87, it was sugar. It got to the situation, where, as there was no sugar, it wasn't worth buying strawberries for jam, so they were just thrown away instead of being brought into the towns.'

'Do you usually have candles on a birthday cake?' 'We have had enough of a problem getting the cake, let alone candles!'

'For a nursery place, what you do is put your name down for your child straight away and join the queue. Sometimes it happens that the child actually gets into the ordinary school before a place comes up in a nursery.'

Misha and his friend sometimes do public paper sales of *Moscow News*, instead of the 'unofficial' journals which they support. Undoubtedly, this 'official' paper is full of critical articles. The authorities allow these, and yet they don't let you get hold of British newspapers.

'If Gorbachev comes under attack,' we ask them, 'and Ligachev or another hard-liner is the alternative, would Gorbachev get the necessary support?' 'Yes, but people prefer Yeltsin.'

Internal passports

Oleg gave us more details of their campaign against both the internal passport system and against the draft. 'We have a passport system. Everyone has an allotted place to live and, to move to anywhere else, you need to have a new permit. It is very, very difficult to get one. For example, I wanted to live in Tallinn but was told I couldn't because I didn't have a permit. You can get a permit to come to Moscow but you would be expected to do the hardest, lowest paid work if you were coming in from outside. You would be a *limitchik*. At first, you would have a temporary permit – for a year or two years. Once you'd been here for four or five years, and provided you hadn't done anything illegal, you would be able to get a permanent permit. But that still doesn't guarantee you anywhere to live.'

'Many workers are forced to live in hostels – barrack-like buildings. The smallest rooms have two people in them. Bigger ones have 16. One, half the size of a normal living room, could have three families living in it – ten square metres in total. Hostels are tied to the workplaces. Two million live in such accommodation in Moscow alone. The paper *Argumenti y Facti* thinks that half a million live in stations, etc.

'Each person who joins our campaign declares a number of things, including that they don't believe in the "Bright Future" promised by the Communist government! We all renounce citizenship in solidarity with those who are not allowed it.

'Our campaign also takes up the abuse of psychiatry. We try to organise meetings, but we are not allowed to. The main aim of our campaign is freedom of movement. The declaration of the rights of man, Article 13, outlines the right of every human being to live where they want. This was signed by the USSR. It is a charter of the United Nations, but it is not implemented here. You can go to a post office to apply for permission to move and they won't talk to you, they won't listen, they send you away.'

Against the draft

Oleg and his mate, who has been applying for some time now to emigrate to the United States, are also campaigning against the draft. This is obligatory for everyone for between two and three years, provided they are not illiterate. They can be jailed for refusing or be sent to a psychiatric hospital.

As the national struggles become more and more acute, there is an ever-growing number of youth who are saying they won't join up to fight their own people, or, sometimes, that they won't join up to fight other people's battles.

Soldiers are organising in a trade union called 'Shield'. Their meetings, which include parents and relatives as well as officers, have been addressed by the most popular liberal deputies like Gdlyan and Sakharov, who have appealed to them not to allow themselves to be used against workers fighting for democratic rights.

The attempt to call up reserves to fight in Azerbaijan in January, came up against mass protests which forced a retreat on the part of the government. Of course the Russian bureaucracy is not prepared to give up its hold on society and its domination of the republics. It will use the army, and it will find the forces sooner or later. How long they remain loyal depends predominantly on how powerful the revolutionary movement against the bureaucracy becomes. The experience of the Russian revolutions themselves shows that soldiers will not refuse to go into battle against workers, until they are prepared to go right over to the side of the revolution. But this has happened before, and it will happen again.

'Democratic *Perestroika*'

At the Institute of Economics and Mathematics, we are guests of a 'Democratic *Perestroika*' club. At least one member of this group is a self-avowed Menshevik! The main subject for discussion is how to stand candidates and put them forward for election.

There is little or no political discussion or even discussion of a programme. Some reports of visits are made and one or two of the leading lights have travelled to Britain, Italy and elsewhere. They have discussed with Willy Brandt on his visit to Moscow and obviously aspire in the direction of social democracy. The only thing they seem to want to know from us is what song is sung at the end of the meetings of the Second International. We presume it must be the *Internationale*. 'Oh how awful! The words are so frightful!'

On the way to the Metro, we discussed with one loyal Party member who wanted to maintain the uphill struggle of trying to reform the Party. He told us that members are leaving at the rate of 300,000 per year. 'I stay here because it would be no good if only the right-wingers were left,' he explains, sadly but helplessly.

When we had been waiting for the meeting to begin, one of the Democratic *Perestroikists* had expressed his worries at the possibilities of civil war. He was unsure if present developments would lead to the 'Hungarian' or the 'Chinese' road. As an economic scientist, how did he do his job, we asked, with no access to Western newspapers? 'With great difficulty,' he replied. 'We know that there are no truly accurate statistics. We doubt everything!'

But what do all these bulging Institutes in Moscow come up with? What do all these academics do – what do they discuss?

Street Life

A visit to a supermarket emphasises the starkness of life. It is in one of those sprawling outskirts of Moscow, surrounded by high rise blocks of flats. The refrigerated display units are literally empty apart from some half kilos of butter that cost 1.75 roubles each. A basket of sausage at 2.90 a kilo is tipped into one of the racks and shoppers appear from nowhere in a scramble.

Milk is 30 kopecks a litre; *kefir* 25 kopecks; tins of fish are 58 kopecks; sardines 1.40 roubles a kilo. Crates in the middle of the floor hold brown paper packages of anything from rice and sugar to flour and lentils. There is no sign of soap or washing up liquid or washing powder. In the fruit and vegetable department, there are bags of apples, potatoes, some cabbages and little else.

We still haven't seen an orange or a grapefruit. We have seen green bananas once and then only available from an impromptu store outside a Metro station. A big queue had formed for these and stocks ran out rapidly, as old women filled up bag after bag – 20 roubles worth of supplies, either for their families or for reselling at some kind of profit.

At another Metro station, a wet-fish stall attracts a massive crowd. Here, as on many street corners, hot pies are plentiful – sweet and savoury – and ice creams, too. But they don't exactly make for a healthy diet!

Metro stations are remarkable, both for their elaborate designs and decor, their brightness and their cleanliness. Women with besoms – twig brushes – are constantly sweeping the dust on the stairs. They pick up cigarette ends and the tiniest pieces of paper. Others sit in little sentry boxes at the bottom of the escalators watching and waiting – part of an inflated workforce or vital for safety and security?

The frequency of the trains is very impressive. An electronic indicator on each platform says how long it is since the last train. Seldom did we see it go over three or four minutes. Usually, it was as little as one and a half or two minutes. Nevertheless, when they came, they were still jam-packed. So were the trams, the trolley-buses and the ordinary buses. In general, the Russian people seem very gentle, but when it comes to travelling, the elbows grow very large and powerful and the language turns quite strong, too!

Perhaps it is in an attempt to moderate the behaviour of travellers that is behind the strange practice of playing radio keep fit programmes over the loud speakers in the stations! How you are expected to respond to instructions and music and 'One, two, three, four' going down those escalators we never fathomed.

The youth are neat and tidy and resourceful. The old are tired and sullen. Many shop workers and public service workers are grumpy and rude. Life hasn't much to offer them, so why should they smile, bow and scrape?

On 27 October, we read belatedly of the murder of a miners' leader in the Donbas. Our hatred towards this regime comes to the surface. Gorky Street is long and it has many monuments and plaques marking historic buildings and events. Haunted by the news from the Ukraine, and seeing the balcony from which Lenin spoke in 1919 in honour of Rosa Luxemburg and Karl Liebknecht, tears of anger well up. The horror of the murder of these revolutionary leaders mingles with the realisation that it can still happen today and tomorrow. Things must change – and rapidly!

The movement on the streets

WHILE IN MOSCOW, we had a discussion with people who had formed a New Socialist Committee (NSC). They want to set up a new socialist party, but at first had to be contented with a 'Committee'. They say they base themselves on Trotsky's ideas, but they have a very long and complicated programme with references to misleading ideas like 'revolutionary reform' and 'municipalisation' – the transfer of state property to the regional or local councils. They say they put forward 'transitional' demands, but had omitted the call for a minimum wage! 'We'll definitely include that', said one of the leaders.

The NSC's leaders tend to regard the Moscow working class as somewhat 'privileged', and therefore less likely than, for example, the miners of the Kuzbas to move into action in the early stages. They may yet be surprised!

They firmly dismiss the idea that the working class of the Soviet Union would ever allow the transfer of the economy into the hands of the capitalists. Nor would the regime, they believe, be able to implement martial law. One of them told us of a recent opinion poll held in October 1989 that showed 35 per cent of the population 'favourable' for Gorbachev. Sixty six per cent of members of the Party apparatus were 'favourable'. This is interesting. It means two-thirds of the population already regarded him unfavourably.

At a 'New Socialist' meeting, mostly of students and held in the massive University building on Lenin Hills, one of their leaders spoke of the need to seek 'alliances with all forces really interested in changing society'. Terms like 'bureaucracy' and 'management', he said, should be avoided, because they are used in the official press.'The possibility of counter-revolution should not be discounted. The "liberal" intelligentsia is trying to make reforms that do not touch the base . . . On the other hand, the "conservatives" will try to hang on to everything.'

Feelings of despair – and hope!

At one stage, we took a brief look into an ancient church where a double funeral was about to take place. The coffins lay open with their occupants completely at peace. The church was full of icons. Women kissed them obsessively, kneeling on the ground and muttering incessantly. If this is their only solace – in a so-called 'socialist' country – their only escape from the drudgery of the daily round – it is a poor reflection on how little progress has been made!

One evening, some of the 'Democratic *Perestroikists*' we have met insist we discuss further with them. It is obvious that the idea of coalition is gaining currency. It also appears that the Komsomol have a number of different wings – Social Democrats, Euro-Communist and at least two 'liberal' factions. But nothing seems to have saved them from an ignominious decline. It is virtually compulsory to join the official youth movement, yet, according to a report in the British *Economist*, in the past four years 11 million have deserted it – in the past year alone four million.

An eminent professor of economics and a 'left' accompanied us on the Metro. He had been puzzling over the great problems of society for decades. Now, he insisted that 'family farms' would be a step forward – so much thinking and such useless conclusions! How much more profound, by contrast, is the wisdom of workers, fashioned in the struggle for existence!

'Revolution on the way!'

The following morning at breakfast, a Ukrainian talked of his homeland. He had come back to it for the first time since being driven out of the country. 'The Ukrainians don't want to separate altogether. But, for example, in sport they want to represent their own nation. If the authorities would just allow them to use their churches, their own language, then things would be OK.

'The miners could bring down the government. There have been big demonstrations recently in the Ukraine and there is no going back. If they try to use the old methods, they won't succeed.' In his opinion, Gorbachev is more popular than Yeltsin still, and he is supported by the nations abroad. 'But undoubtedly a revolution is on the way.' *This was over breakfast in a tourist hotel!*

That morning, we went to a small park, where all the unofficial groups gather on Sundays. A meeting with speakers would be illegal. A few police kept an eye on the proceedings. Queues formed in snakes through the crowd for each 'unofficial' paper as it was brought out of a seller's bag. Leaflets were snapped up and crowds gathered round newspaper cuttings pasted up on the side of a kiosk.

Regardless of the rules, once a debate opened up between ourselves and the editor of a well-known *samizdat, Expres-Chronik*, most of the people in the park gathered round us. They wanted to hear what these English socialists had to say, but they also wanted to put their point of view. We were besieged with pleas to take up heart-rending miscarriages of justice and to work miracles.

One woman was in tears as she described how she had been thrown out of her job with the state television because she dared to criticise the management. Another woman asked us to take up the unfair treatment of an artist. His work depicted the struggle against fascism – of Soviet prisoners in Nazi concentration camps, as he himself was, or in Chile. Despite being one of the leaders of the revolt in Buchenwald, he was imprisoned on his return to the Soviet Union in 1946, then released and rehabilitated in 1958. His health is now suffering, he cannot get anywhere decent to live and he had been denied a war pension. There are thousands, perhaps hundreds of thousands, like him.

Yet another woman asked what defence we had in Britain against the use of psychiatric hospitals to detain political dissidents. A man with a grotesquely distorted arm – a mangled wrist – spoke of the treatment he had received at the hands of the state during a period of imprisonment.

People were investing their last hopes of salvation in us as if, because we came from a distant, unfamiliar land, we had magical powers. We had appeared in their lives like spacemen from another planet where things must be better. The ones reported in the official press, by the way, had no sooner landed than they started singing the praises of *Perestroika* and *Glasnost*!

An engineering worker

We had an afternoon rendezvous with an engineering worker at the famous Gorky Park. Stepan told us stories of the March election campaign when the old stooges had failed to gain the qualifying 50 per cent. One got as little as 25 per cent! They had held meetings everywhere.

Workers in Moscow may be better off, with higher bonuses, slightly more food available, etc. But, when it came to the elections in March, they had to struggle to get any of the people they wanted into the Congress of Deputies. Against all the odds, they had got Vlasov in, for example. Stepan had been delighted at the results! In the summer, like so many others he knew, he had taken two weeks off work to watch the new Deputies debating in the televised Congress.

Stepan agreed to arrange for us to meet a number of car workers and others at his flat three days later. The meeting unfortunately was never to take place. Within twenty-four hours, on Political Prisoners' Day, Stepan would be arrested and held for two weeks for participating in the Pushkin Square protests.

Another confused man!

Pavel works in Moscow, for a group called the Information Centre. 'Wood and timber from Siberia are sent to the Ukraine to be made into furniture and then back to Siberia,' he says. 'And people there are producing hydro-electric power, which is not needed in that place. If the wood, the energy, the timber, etc., had a price, this sort of inefficiency wouldn't happen. People are looking for solutions at the level of the enterprise. But that is only possible when the state allows the cities and enterprises to decide what they want to produce and to buy stock.'

Pavel thought the miners had shown a certain incompetence, 'Especially in relation to the co-ops, which they condemned. Then they demanded the right to fix their own prices and to decide who to sell their coal to. In other words they were opposed to the market for others, but in favour of it for themselves.'

The strikes in Vorkuta, and the Kuzbas and elsewhere, he told us, were still continuing. 'We'll be in for a hard winter. They are demanding a higher income in the steel industry, transport, etc., though they are not producing any more. Producing less under the economic reforms than before is leading to high inflation, as well as a shortage of goods. Unorganised workers are in a very difficult position.

'Some workers are taking strike action, others operating boycotts, go-slows etc. Electricity, central heating, water have all been affected by such disruption.'

Pavel had been a member of a *Perestroika* Club in 1988 and still had links with 'Democratic *Perestroika*'. He had been a dissident in the '60s, '70s and '80s – imprisoned for setting up a library of banned literature. He reckoned he had got off lightly, more lightly than others: 'Just 13 months with the KGB and one year in the "madhouse". I got on well with the doctors so I was spared the worst of the treatment.'

After his release, for years he was followed. He could only work as a loader, doing manual work, or as a store-man. He was chased out of various jobs. He was an economist at one of the Institutes and he should have qualified for a diploma, but he was thrown out. Some people who have spent years in mental hospitals are only now being released.

The Lubyanka Prison

On our way to the Political Prisoners' Day protest, we passed by the Lenin museum. Lo and behold! In the space where we had seen that electors' meeting just a few days before, a giant scaffolding-type 'sculpture' has now appeared, concreted to the pavement. What a blatant attempt to prevent people congregating in this area. It's a bit like the giant (and futile) flower boxes put on Brixton's pavements straight after the disturbances of 1981.

A big crowd is gathering in Dzerzhinsky Square opposite the KGB headquarters – hell-house for so many as the notorious Lubyanka prison. The police begin to block off access to the building where a human chain is forming. Candles are being lit and encircled with paper to protect them against the wind.

We make our way under the fence across six lanes of traffic and then round to the front gate of the headquarters where the camera spotlights are blazing.

After the allotted half hour – agreed with the KGB – the 'vigil' disperses. Many go in the direction of Pushkin Square, where a further protest demonstration has been called. We arrive there only to find this favourite meeting place suddenly closed to the people. Crowds gather on every pavement and in every side street.

A rumour spreads that Sakharov is about to speak. In the event, it is the poet, Yevtushenko. But no one imagines any speaker will last long, given the van loads of the hated *SpetsNats* – the paramilitary police – waiting alongside them. A few forays are made by these 'armed bodies of men'. They are hissed and booed (and photographed) every time they make an appearance. They come out of the vans to let fly and crack a few skulls and go back in again.

There are acts of dare-devil defiance – youths mounting telephone boxes to wave the flag of February etc. There are scuffles and skirmishes and then many arrests. A Russian worker who speaks German takes it on himself to protect me from the police. 'As a foreigner, they will be very interested in you,' he announced

The SpetsNats!

'Down with the Partocracy!'

rather disconcertingly. With quiet determination, he actually put himself between me and the forces of the state as I dodged about taking incriminating photographs of the white-helmeted enemy. We chatted about politics. This man had voted for Yeltsin, but he was not so sure now; he thought he was a bit of an adventurist.

The *SpetsNats*

Later, we discovered that another acquaintance of ours, apart from Stepan the engineer, had been arrested and held that night. After his release, he described what happened:

'There must have been anything from 5-8000 in the different streets around, unable to get into Pushkin Square. It was completely different this year from last year. The police were quite polite. The militia men are actually interested in politics now, but the *SpetsNats* were sent in in buses and stopped right in front of us. They can be guaranteed to attack. In the court where I was, 56 cases came up and I am certain that there were at least 100 altogether.

'The evidence against me was fabricated. They accused me of shouting one of the slogans of the Democratic Union, which I would not do. I was nearly 24 hours in the cell on remand, with no food. Some of those arrested and tried at the height of the battles got an immediate ten or fifteen day sentence. If you don't have a passport on you, you can be kept for three days, otherwise the legal maximum is supposed to be only three hours. At 7.00pm on the following evening, I was tried in a tiny room. I was threatened with 15 days' detention.

'"When will you stop calling meetings which are not authorised?" "When the totalitarian regime is in ruins!" I replied.'

'I was asked about an arrest in December 1988. They also said I had been arrested by three people together; hardly likely. I was supposed to have shouted "fascist!". I was fined 200 roubles.'

Moscow meeting with miners

Grapefruit hit the streets on 31 October, but we didn't have time to stop and buy them! We had discussions planned with members of an independent union – and were to meet miners based in Moscow. They were from the Ukraine, but participating in the permanent commission set up to implement the summer 'protocol' – the massive list of concessions that had ended the historic summer strike.

Leonid from Donetzk explained that there are representatives from the six major coal fields on the commission. The union finances them. 'But it's a disgrace,' he says. 'The lion is the king of the animals, but he doesn't have to have a formal status to prove it. Men have enormous strength but have to seek official status before it is recognised.

'Our committees are very young and impatient. We very much liked the message from Terry Fields that was sent through during our strike. The only reason you didn't get a reply, was because we didn't have agreement on our Strike Committee as to what to say!'

Sergei, Leonid's fellow miner, said he wanted to ask us a 'theoretical question of Marxism'. 'What is the aristocracy of labour?' After one sentence of a reply – which was not all that needed to be said – he moved on to the next question: 'How should we approach the question of alternative work to mining?' Us: 'Insist on it. But it cannot be seen except in the context of the struggle for genuine socialism – workers' control and management of a plan to provide suitable jobs when and where they are needed'

Leonid and **Sergei**: 'Miners seem to be the backbone of every country's labour movement. Why is this? Where do they get their power from?' 'What laws could be drawn up ensuring that new working practices and new equipment are adopted?' 'Shouldn't the miners be able to decide on these things?'

Leonid: 'There are different wings of our Committee. The conservatives are for working in the official unions. At first we thought along those lines, then we concluded "no". The situation is opening up and we are looking to build our own union, but we need help. Each mining area is working on its own. It is proving very difficult to bring together a national organisation. We want to know how to proceed.'

In a few sentences, we tried to sum up a programme that would help to build these new unions. A programme of basic demands that are common to all regions could surely be drawn up to unite all the coal fields. But Leonid and his comrade seemed to have just one doubt about our programme: 'It would not work because workers are not literate enough!' They felt that, although the Vorkuta miners were putting forward more social and political demands on behalf of all miners, the Donbas was suffering from having no cultural or intellectual leaders.

Workers' confidence

The first thing for these workers is to have confidence in themselves, and in the mighty power they can wield to change society.

Intellectuals can be helpful, especially if they put themselves on the stand point of the working class. But no section of workers, genuinely trying to forge the fighting weapons of struggle have to wait for an outside force of intellectuals to provide them with a finished programme.

In his pamphlet *What is to be Done*, Lenin made some comments in criticising the 'Economists' which he later corrected. He argued that workers were only capable of a trade union consciousness, whereas the intelligentsia would take Marxist ideas into the working class. He wrote later, in *12 Years*, that he had bent the stick too far in arguing against the Economists. They had a mechanical, passive approach, insisting that workers would automatically come to a correct programme on the basis of their own experience of events – all that was necessary was to concentrate on trade union struggles. Marxist ideas are not alien to the working class, coming from 'outside'. They are rooted in the very experience of the workers themselves. The role of Marxists is to make conscious the unconscious strivings of the working class, and to generalise their experience. But this can and has been done on many occasions by workers drawing their own conclusions.

Unfortunately, general ideas are sometimes put in a vague and abstract manner and can initially receive no echo of response. We heard that, in Siberia, a poet had attempted to discuss with miners the most abstract ideas of Hegel, but in the heat of the struggle had not been very well received. But socialists attempting to build an independent organisation of workers must encourage the study of theoretical questions as well as issues such as the management of industry and the role of the trade unions – as long as they are linked to the concrete questions that workers face.

The basics of Marxist theory cannot be evaded. The aspiring trade union leaders we were with admitted to us, 'No one is clear, even what socialism is!'

Women's lot

Sofia is unemployed. She gave up her job as a geologist because she felt her talents and qualifications were simply not being used. She was expected to sit doing nothing all day. 'I have a terror of going to hospital because they have no sterile instruments. People end up going to the private health groups – co-ops – where they have to pay for treatment, simply because there they know they will have their own syringe and no one else has used it before and no one will use it afterwards.

'There are two kinds of hospital: one with everything you need and the rest. Ordinary, simple people only get to the ordinary, simple hospital. The first category hospitals are for the people of the government and their families, their brothers, their sisters. They all get the service free, although they earn big money. Our hospitals are dirty and short of medicines. Some syringes are used 30 times over. We have the horror of new-born children getting AIDS and dying as a result. I know two women who died when their children were born. Many children die before they are one year old.

'You ask if it is true that women have as many as three abortions. A friend of mine has had six and no one thinks it's unusual. In Moscow, at least they use anaesthetics when they carry out abortions. But in the provinces, there is no anaesthetic and the women suffer terrible pain.

'People say that Russian women are very strong. They go through fire and great difficulties. Women even build the railways. You see old women in yellow jackets with large hammers constructing the tracks. They are old, tired and often very ill. They are not forced to do these jobs, literally. But, for example, if their husbands drink a lot because of working hard and low pay, they have to take jobs like this to maintain the family. In the little towns, they can't find easier work for women because the wives of all the high officials have all those jobs.'

In the course of the Russian revolution of 1917, it was the women who played a key role; the February revolution itself exploded on International Women's Day. From the women we met, and the discussions we had, it is clear that once again, women will be in the forefront of the battles to come.

State repression

WE MET BORIS, a worker who gives a large part of his spare time to the organisation *Memorial*.

'There are three strands to *Memorial's* work. Firstly the historical – collecting the material in the archives – unpublished material, throwing light onto the history of repression.

'The second is welfare work for those who survived the repression of the '30s, '40s, '50s, and '60s. We give practical help, medical help, legal help. Thirdly is the socio-political strand. Our programme is similar to that of the dissidents of the '70s – against arbitrariness, lawlessness, injustice. We embrace many political strands of opinion.

'Last year we held our first National Conference. We want recognition for *Memorial* and justice for the relations of all victims of political repression.

'We have members in 180 cities, and we aim to produce a bulletin.

'The KGB know where the mass graves are, but they hide information. Eventually it comes to light. There are two particular cemeteries in Moscow where we know the victims of repression have been buried. The bodies used to be brought to the Crematorium at Donsky from the Lubyanka Prison, and the ashes scattered there. Now we have little monuments at both cemeteries.

'We are worried that young people don't know what happened in the past. We want the KGB files opened and all the necessary information collected. Even if we got rid of the Lubyanka, and transformed the KGB, there would still be problems for a long time yet.

'My grandfather was arrested in 1938 and shot in a camp. My grandmother suffered terribly, and this was transmitted to the family. It is not the only reason why I give my time to *Memorial*. It is in order to get rid of the atmosphere of fear of repression. Everyone still feels the horrors inside. But we have no press no publications, no premises and resources . . . Only enthusiasm.'

95

Georgi is a member of *Memorial* who collects as much of Trotsky's material as he can lay his hands on – his books, articles, photographs etc. His keen interest stems from his early reading of some works by Trotsky, by which he was extremely impressed, but also from curiosity about the disappearance of his grandfather.

He was a party member who had been overheard on a bus cracking a joke with his work-mates. This was in 1937. He was asked who he would be voting for in the elections and laughed, 'Comrade Trotsky of course!' He had not arrived home from work when the Party men came for him. They left a message with his wife to tell him to come to the Party committee.

Dutifully he went there; but he never came back! He was never seen again by his family. They sent letters and parcels, but never knew whether anything reached him. They think he was probably put to work building canals in one of Stalin's numerous forced labour camps. He was officially rehabilitated in 1960, and probably died some time after that . . . without trace.

Georgi's mother explained:

'We were made to believe it was a shameful event to even mention our father. He was labelled an "enemy of the people". We had been brought up to suppose that the secret police never made a mistake. If you considered complaining you were asked if you disapproved of the secret police. "Don't you trust us? Ahaa, an interesting person. We will have to find out more about you."

'There were millions who disappeared like our father – millions. He was a jolly fellow, liked to joke. He was a Southern man – happy, jovial. He would never get involved in trouble. Always helped people who had suffered.'

At one stage in the 1940s, the secret police had tried to involve Georgi's mother in their operations. They had a quota to fulfil of how many they should recruit to the service. They tried to soften her up by blaming her for not having 'patriotic feelings'. 'I wasn't reading the papers, they said. I had my head full of the story about Fedeyev's novel in which the heroine is a military translator and that is all I was interested in doing. I applied and reapplied to the various Institutes. I was told I would have to leave Moscow.

'One day, someone came up secretively and took me into an office. They reminded me of my father and asked if I wanted to serve the Motherland. I was eighteen years old, and had been fed on stories of girls winning great acclaim for denouncing their fathers etc., and risking their lives if they didn't.

'I was asked to look into the circumstances of a friend of mine who had lost her father and uncle during the war. They tried to influence people who were vulnerable. I was naive and they tried to play on my emotions. Eventually they left me in peace because I was *too* naive. Since then I have come to understand about the KGB and now I hate them. For 70 years, people have been living isolated lives. We have a society of "Banditism".'

Georgi's mother, who was of the opinion that it has been all downhill since Peter the Great, obviously harked back to a golden age. Everything was 'heroic' before the revolution. But in her hatred for the present bandits at the head of society, she was blinded to the heroic age of the Russian revolution itself. The original forerunner of the KGB, the Cheka, had been set up by some of the most devoted, most incorruptible, most self-sacrificing of class fighters. These were not blood-thirsty fiends, as they have been portrayed many times since then. By contrast, the NKVD, the GPU and the KGB itself drew support from the dregs of society.

The Cheka had been a necessary instrument for defence against counter-revolutionary terrorist groups, to secure the survival of the government which, for the first time in history, was based on the rule of the majority. Its role was to suppress the armed capitalist counter-revolution. Those terror organisations – the GPU, NKVD, KGB – which mushroomed after Stalin had usurped power were given as their main task the brutal persecution and extermination of the flower of the revolutionary movement. First and foremost amongst their victims were the followers of Trotsky and the Left Opposition. Their crimes will be avenged. So too will the suffering of all those dragged into the whirlpool of the purges.

Georgi's father's father had been an officer in the Tsar's navy. He had become a Bolshevik, and worked in the Ministry of Oil shipments in the Caspian sea. He, too, had been arrested in 1930, held for nine months and lost his job. Georgi's father was a stoker – a Greek and a Bolshevik. Georgi explained about the arbitrariness of Stalin's purges: 'The figure for the numbers to be destroyed in an area would be issued to the secret police and the Party. "Evict a hundred peasants – in this village, ten; in this village, seven; etc." In the border regions, foreigners were considered as potential traitors, and therefore particularly singled out for persecution. Many were accused of Trotskyism.

'Trotsky was popular at that time. Posters of him were put up on demonstrations in factories and in the camps.' Another member of Georgi's family had been a partisan and sunk a German boat, but he had ended up betrayed and executed. His mother's family had got the last train out of Mariupol, on the shores of the Azov Sea. It was then bombed by the Germans. She had seen for herself the epaulettes of the nurses and doctors at the station as they pulled out. These were Germans!

Lenin and Trotsky

'A few meetings have already been called by *Memorial* to commemorate the lives of persecuted Bolsheviks,' Georgi informed us. 'For example, at the Aviation Institute there was one meeting chronicling the life of Trotsky, and another one for Bukharin.

'There have been big meetings recently to protest at the co-ops and price rises. Organisations like the "United Workers' Front" have been formed, stirring up workers against the intellectuals and against the "Independents". They are still in favour of deputies being elected through the factories but workers will not be fooled by their arguments. They are just Stalinists trying to regain their hold at every level of society.

'When candidates were being picked for the elections in March, meetings were disregarded. In one case, the director of a clock-factory was promoted by the apparatus. This Samsonov is a hated, reactionary man, but he got through. He spoke at the Congress of Deputies challenging Popov of the "liberal" wing to come to his factory and show what his programme would mean in practice – taunting him to demonstrate whether he could run a workshop.

'These people are full of demagogic rhetoric, trying to whip up workers against the opposition. Unfortunately, the liberal opposition is strong on criticism of the present regime, but not so strong on recipes for curing the situation. Popov, for example, has devised alternative theories of management to replace the "command system". It seems attractive, but has yet to be proved a practical viability.'

Georgi points out that the 'liberals' who are attacking 'Communism' aim their blows against Trotsky rather than Lenin. 'There are others attempting to defend his record. Boldakiev, a historian of the revolution for example, lectures on Trotsky. Trotsky's calumniators say he exercised summary and arbitrary justice, but Boldakiev says that, in all the archives, not once has he seen an order from Trotsky to "arrest and shoot". It was always: "Where necessary, arrest and put on trial", or "Arrest and court-martial".'

Georgi traces the present bureaucratically-run, centralised society to Lenin's idea that – in his words – 'Society has to be like one big factory in which everyone works with orders given from above'.

What Lenin actually wrote in *State and Revolution* was that, in the first stage of communist society:

> ... All citizens become employees and workers of a single countrywide state syndicate ... When the majority of the people begin independently and everywhere to keep such accounts and exercise such control over the capitalists (now converted into employees)

and over the intellectual gentry who preserve their capitalist habits, this control will really become universal, general and popular; . . . the whole of society will have become a single office and a single factory, with equality of labour and pay.

But this 'factory' discipline . . . is by no means our ideal, or our ultimate goal . . . From the moment all members of society, or at least the vast majority, have learned to administer the state themselves . . . from this moment the need for government of any kind begins to disappear altogether. The more complete the democracy the nearer the moment when it becomes unnecessary.

A candle-lit vigil at KGB HQ

To the Donbas Coalfield

JUST BEFORE WE set out for Donetzk, we read that the Donbas miners will have just conducted a warning strike on 1 November. Miners at the largest pit in Vorkuta are defying both the law and a reported decision of the Strike Committee in the area, to go on strike. All the miners are fighting for the full implementation of the 'protocol', but also for the political demands of 'An end to Article 6', and for 'the separation of the jobs of the Party leader and the President'. We are obviously on our way to one of the right places!

The view from the window of 'Hotel Miner', Donetzk, is a horizon lined with pit-heaps and pit heads. We can taste coal with every breath we take, yet the town has an air of prosperity. There are wide boulevards, large flower beds, clean streets, big shop fronts, brightly lit cinemas and sports centres. There are banners and posters everywhere in preparation for the Revolution's anniversary celebrations. A massive poster depicting different workers urges the population to 'Put *Perestroika* into action!'

Everywhere are slogans and carvings commemorating the key role that coal miners play in the life of the Soviet Union. Apart from 'Hotel Miner', you have 'Coal Food Store', 'Coal Restaurant', etc.

One of the slogans of the city is 'Without the Donbas, without coal, socialism is an empty phrase.' On the part of the bureaucracy, given the way they have treated the miners – taken them for granted and exploited their labour – this is repellent hypocrisy. As for the miners themselves, they will take pride in the historic role they will undoubtedly play in the future, transforming this closed and unjust society.

Lenin Square looks peaceful. It is difficult to imagine it as it was for nine days last summer, packed full of striking miners camped out in their tents.

Strike Committee HQ

We find eventually the headquarters of the miners' Strike Committee, not now in Lenin Square, as it was during the strike in July, but right in the middle of the equivalent of Coal Board House. It was too late at night for us to find any of the strike committee members in the building, but we tracked down the home of a miner whose name we had read in the British press. Entering a dark doorway, and climbing a dark stairway, confronting a tiny noisy dog, we found the miner's mother . . . but no miner. He was taking a break by the Black Sea. The mother nevertheless engulfs us like lost children, treats us to grapefruit, meat, bread and biscuits and Turkish coffee.

The next day breaks over us like a tidal wave. Just walking into the rooms of the miners' *StachKom* (Strike Committee), you have almost a physical sensation of that motor force which will drive the political revolution forward. We are greeted as if we have all been comrades all our lives! Such is the generosity of spirit of those who feel the world is their oyster. These people feel they have already struck a mighty blow against the dictatorship of the bureaucracy. They also have a strong sense of responsibility, to proceed carefully, without being provoked or launching provocative actions. Theirs could become an unstoppable movement, once the direction it needs to travel becomes clear to all.

We made our introductions and explained what brought us there. Things were happening, phones were going, people were constantly in and out of the rooms. Sasha, Ludmilla, Viktor, Lidia, Kolya and Yuri – leading members of the Strike Committee – made time to discuss with us. They ensured we were booked in for a meal at lunch-time in the Coal Board canteen. Lidia's mother was phoned to prepare a special evening meal for us at her apartment.

They talked non-stop of their lives, their aims, their struggles and their strikes:

'On Wednesday last week – 1 November – all the pits in the area held a two hour warning stoppage and sent representatives to a meeting in Lenin Square. The Oktabrskaya pit was out all day. Further action is under consideration, but striking is always difficult – no pay, and no funds. Even this short strike was illegal. The agreement that ended the summer strike has not been implemented.

'The price we receive for the coal is entirely inadequate to provide new machinery. Most pits don't have the machinery needed, so it means that the work is very hard underground. If the pits don't make money, there's nothing for equipment. Without money, we cannot get cement and timber. We get 24 roubles a ton, and the state sells it for 48. The pits have no money to build accommodation. Miners are having to wait 15-20 years for a flat. There are no materials.

'There is still a big bureaucracy. We want to make sure everything is implemented. Each town has a committee. Each pit sends delegates to the town committee. The pit committees' discussions are brought to Regional level. There are between 8 and 11 members of the city committee – it varies. The strike committee meets about once every ten days, or when the need arises.

'For a long time, the official unions have been under the influence of the management. We need a union that is independent and representing workers. We had a conference with the union and put forward a candidate of the strikers to get someone to head the union, and we got him in – in Donetzk – his name is Ladigin. This was a victory – the first time we have got our own representative in the official union.

'In the past, the management and the Party put forward the candidate. Now, things are different. We want to change the union from top to bottom – get our own leaders at every level, our own structure. We will keep our own committee functioning until this is achieved – if it can be achieved. The same thing applies across the Union – the Kuzbas have their workers' strike committees'.

Ludmilla works in the nursery at the Skotchinskovo pit and is 'released' by the other workers to work at the *StachKom* Headquarters. 'In the past,' she says, 'every candidate had to be a Party member whatever else they were. We want to choose someone because they do a good job.

'Up to now, we have confined ourselves to economic demands. Now we must look further, with political demands. Our union is trying to draw in other workers – metal workers, kolkhoz workers ... It is not a *trade* union, but an independent movement of *all* workers. We are setting up a movement which elects "our people" and is capable of achieving real popular power ... like in the Kuzbas, where the workers' strike committees put forward their own candidates for election – in the Party, at City level and up to the Supreme Soviets.

'We have a council of the workers' collectives. Other workers agree to cover our jobs while we do the *StachKom* work. We don't collect dues for our organisation – we still have to pay the official union. But we collect voluntary donations for special things, like journeys away, etc.' They have the use of rooms, telephones, canteen, and typing equipment in the Coal Board HQ. They have the use of the Conference Hall as well. They had got these facilities because of the power they demonstrated during the strike. Sasha emphasised this by banging the table with his fist – a big man with a big fist!

Elections

Ludmilla: 'In every area, commissions are preparing for the elections to get what they want at every level. In Donetzk, the Union of Electors involves workers and professionals like teachers – informal organisations and illegal ones also – to fight the Party apparatus and anyone else who hinders what they are doing.'

Sasha: 'We are not simply and solely anti-Party, but in this poll, we were just told "Here's your candidate". People just voted and didn't say anything. The task of the Union of Electors is to wake people up so that they don't stay quiet and so that we get representatives to fight for ordinary workers' interests and no longer people who don't represent their interests. Of course, they could still be members of the Party.

'The authorities are afraid of us, but we still have some problems. They would not let us have a microphone and loudspeakers for last Wednesday's meeting. The Government wants to operate *Perestroika* from above; we are doing it from below. *Perestroika* is going too slowly and things are getting worse.

'It is not so much that people were afraid, but we were taught for so long to wait and be patient. The fear of war and hunger was certainly very deep in their consciousness, because of their bitter experiences. As long as things were getting better, there was hope; when that changed, the dam burst. They could see we were patient. We believed in the "Brighter Future" under Stalin, Khrushchev, Brezhnev, and so on. That's what we were looking forward to.

'Now people's psychology is that they are going to create soviet power themselves. What we have seen with the People's Soviet (the Congress of People's Deputies and the Supreme Soviet) is new. We had not expected such a development. In the past, any idiot could be at the rostrum and people would just clap indifferently. Now they can't get away with that kind of thing.

'Before, we never imagined we could put ourselves forward as candidates. Before it would be: "We need a candidate. Got to be a woman/a worker/such and such an age". Now, we can decide and discuss with the candidates what we want. There is still a long way to go. There are differences in consciousness in the cities and the other mining areas. Schevchenko, for example, got in on the city vote and social organisations. In Kiev, it's different from here.'

We asked how people felt when Sherbitsky (the Brezhnevite Regional Party boss) was removed. Both Sasha and Ludmilla answered in unison: 'Indifferent. Everybody thought he had died long ago anyway!'

The July 1989 Strike

We asked if they had received a letter from the British Labour MP Terry Fields, who had sent a message of support to the strike in the summer. Ludmilla: 'Yes, it was read out in the square to the thousands of miners there.' And what about the programme in that message which meant that, if everyone was involved in government as Sasha described it, there would be no place for 'specialists' with their own 'apparatus' or state machine?

Lidia: 'It is a very important thing that workers have control themselves. In the past, there was no accountability. People want to be able to check on their representatives after a day or a year. The people at the top get big privileges but don't work. We want an end to all privileges.'

'The strike in the summer really developed from the Kuzbas. People were fed up with waiting. Before then, there had been individual strikes. It spread to Karaganda in Kazakhstan, then north. The government went to the Kuzbas and offered a few totally inadequate crumbs – and the strike immediately spread to the rest of the Soviet Union. Conditions might be worst in the Kuzbas, but they are bad everywhere and we needed to fight for all miners. Holidays and pensions were amongst our main demands, and there were other general ones. But each area had its own, local demands – supporting certain deputies, calling for particular resources. *(See list of printed demands in appendix)*

'It wasn't just a quick walk-out. Each pit had meetings to discuss and work out the demands and only after that, they came out. Every pit sent delegates to see the Party Committee in the Square. We put forward 47 demands.

'We were in the Lenin Square from 19-24 July, night and day. The miners had decided enough was enough. They were not going to stay quiet any longer. We went to the Square, put forward our demands, and waited for a reply.

Good news, bad news

At this point, our discussion was interrupted by the news from a phone call that the miners' own committees or 'union' had been recognised as a *bona fide* organisation. A victory! **But** there was also news that eight of the Donetzk miners' leaders had received warning letters from the authorities for organising an 'illegal demonstration/meeting' in the Square on 1 November.

They were indignant, because the Party Secretary and other

'leading lights' had participated. (The Party Secretary and a policeman had attended the *StachKom* meeting the next day, though there were protests half way through the meeting.) There was also a bit of a flurry of activity around sending a telegram of protest about a new management body that was being set up for Donetzk Coal. 'It is a bureaucratic organisation and we want it scrapped, not another body that's just the same set up!'

Viktor then joined the discussion.

'The New Law is anti-democratic. It doesn't say it is against strikes. It goes all round the houses avoiding the issue, but what it says on the restriction of action does not accord with the Charter of Human Rights. We saw that in Britain, during the miners' strike, and also in the USA during the airline pilots' strike, the law was used against them. There's no ideal country!'

Sasha came back into the room: '*Our strike is not finished. Our strike continues!*'

Lidia was the only woman strike leader in the Square in July. The wives of the miners didn't get involved – Ludmilla, for example, had to continue her work in the creche.

Lidia: 'At first, there were just economic demands. Miners were not involved in politics. They would go to work, get paid, buy their food. Then they started to think. They began to realise they had heard promises and promises – but no more money came. Now they are standing up for themselves . . . Miners want sausages, soap and good pay!'

Ludmilla earns around 100 roubles a month. She pays 30 roubles a month for her lunches, 15 for her rent and then the rest is for everything else, including clothes. She spent five years underground. It was good money and not very heavy work but wet and clammy. She worked on a machine operating the transport, which is the best job for women but a very responsible job. Women don't work underground now in the Donetzk area, although a few do in the north.

'On 25 October, Vorkuta started striking again for political demands. The Donbas is supporting them. We want to get rid of Article 6 of the constitution on the leading role of the Communist Party. We want direct elections of the chairs of the Soviets at every level. We are not convinced we *will* get free elections, but that's what we are fighting for. And separation of the President and General Secretary of the Party. We want confirmation of the status of the workers' movement – free Unions.'

She added 'We want a second workers' party.' She was not a member of the Party – 'But Ludmilla is. Quite discredited!' – and they both laughed. Lidia: 'I hate them! Though I know Ludmilla is a good worker and she is a good friend of mine. Things are still the same, they don't improve. On the one side, you have the working class. On the other, you have the *mafia*.' Ludmilla: 'I will stay in the Party – it's *my* Party – but I do think we need another party, too.'

Control Commissions

The two women told us that Viktor, who had now left us, was a very popular man. 'He is a miner, but is taking on the *mafia* – as a member of the Workers' Control Commission.

'The domination of everything from the top, including all enterprises, leads to corruption and the creation of a *mafia*. The Workers' Control Commission exposes things like people making false claims as invalids for money not due to them. There is a "People's Control" – a Party body. People get paid for being on it, but they don't do anything, so we have our own "Workers' Control".

'Crime **did** fall sharply during the strike. It had been increasing before that. The police noted it, too! Our "control" took on the functions of the police. The Strike Committee sent a letter to the authorities, saying "We're responsible for all policing. We will be in full control of the town".'

Kolya joined in: 'During the strike, while everyone was in the square we actually had a tape around the demo, as a form of protection. When we have a meeting in normal circumstances, anyone can speak, but when the strike was on, we said that no one from outside can be allowed to come in. We were wary of any kind of provocation or anything that could upset the delicate balance at that stage.

'This is the first time people have stood up in 70 years so they didn't dare let the police loose because there would have been civil war! We organised pickets and banned alcohol. The government sent its commission to ask what we wanted. They were terrified we would put forward political demands. We made a big mistake during the strike when other workers came to us and we just said, "We have our own demands and that's it". After all, everyone is affected by the *mafia*.'

Yuri arrived and took us into another office. As one of the leaders who called the strike on 1 November, he had received a letter:

Illegal action

'We are being told that we have broken Article 185 – 1 AK of the "Administrative Code" of the USSR. Next time it will be a fine of 200 roubles, and if there's another time – 1,000 roubles, and two month's "administrative detention" – working wherever the authorities decide, with 20 per cent of wages being taken by the state.' While talking to us, he was trying to get through to a Narodny Front lawyer in Moscow, who didn't seem able to understand anything. Yuri put the phone down in exasperation.

'The Government Commission has said it accepts all 47 demands, but they are not being implemented. There are delays, and things are being turned upside down and on their head. We have been passing resolutions, organising protests and demonstrations. Now we are on full "Strike Alert".

'Eleven out of the 13 pits in Vorkuta are now on indefinite strike. One pit is the solid hard core for the action. The press has tried to say the others aren't out, but it isn't true.'

Then, eight miners from Mezhdurechensk were ushered in to have a look at us. They sat down in a row facing us, took their caps off and sat with them on their knees. 'What do you know about our strike?' For a few minutes, we discussed a number of things: the solidarity campaign, exchange visits of miners. Yuri said they were not keen on superficial visits, but wanted to send a Ukrainian miner to work in a British pit for a month.

'We have decided to produce a newspaper, but we lack facilities, paper, etc. – the authorities won't allow us any.'

The Mezhdurechensk miners, apparently satisfied with what they'd heard and with a long journey to make, left the room.

Yuri: 'In our "Charter", the main aim is the democratic running of society. The miners' agreement can't be fulfilled on the basis of the present system. Fulfilling it means changing the system. Gorbachev's aim is to move from the administrative "command system" to sound economic principles. This is our main task. Everyone agrees in general, but when it gets to concrete questions, the Government and the Coal Board still approach everything in the spirit of the administrative command system.

'The new devaluation should mean we can sell more coal abroad, but there is a limit of 3 per cent on exports of coal. West Germany buys washed coal at $40 a ton, and Turkey unwashed at $20, so we could get between 120 roubles and 250 roubles per ton. But in Donetzk we get between 24 and 70 at the most, and they – central government – get 48 roubles as a minimum. The price is arbitrarily fixed by some civil servant signing a bit of paper. We want to take from the Ministry the right to dispose of our coal.

'Point 24 deals with Sundays – the right not to work. The plan lays down that we should produce 933,000 tons, but without Sundays it would be 833,000, so they just won't implement this point.

Prices and the market

'If we had our way, at first the production of coal would go down, and the price would go up. But then production would pick up and prices go down, through the use of new machinery, etc.'

'Do you agree with the introduction of "market" mechanisms?' we asked. 'Yes.' 'As a solution for the whole economy?'

'No. The market, we know, can cause problems, but we have blockages now and *must* have elements of the market introduced. We can't be dogmatic on economic questions. We are working on the issues. Things may be different in the future.

'It's not a question of "Plan" versus "Market". A "Free Market" is not the answer. It's not a question of a name, a label, but of effectiveness.

'The workers' movement here is very young, just three months old and not yet completely politicised. We just wanted to do what was necessary to put ourselves in a better position. At first, any mention of politics was greeted with horror. Now it's accepted. It's because of the objective situation.

'In some places, the STKs have workers and management in them. At the pits, it is only miners. Who you get into positions depends on the atmosphere that exists.'

To be continued . . .

The discussion broke off, to be continued *en route* to the social.

Some of us waited outside a food store while a delegation went inside to buy a cake for the feast. Sasha then produced a badge with the emblem of Vorkuta – a reindeer and pit winding gear. He pinned it to my coat. It was a moving moment for us. We explained that Vorkuta had a special place in our hearts. It was here in the labour camp that the last remnants of the Trotskyist Left Opposition were finally wiped out after heroic resistance. 'That's why they are so militant' Sasha stated simply. 'The spirit of the fight against Stalin lives on in the miners.'

We all then clambered onto a trolley bus. Each time it stopped, we heard loud music coming through the door. It was blaring out of the loud-speakers on every street corner, every building. The population was virtually being instructed to celebrate, to enjoy themselves, to rejoice at the October Revolution. No wonder people get a bit turned off.

Donetzk was once known as Stalino. Some things change; others as yet, do not!

As we walked through Lenin Square, our hosts, the strikers' leaders, told us that when they occupied the square in the summer in the days of the strike, they had declared that Donetzk was 'a city of roses, not of snowdrops' – a city of striking miners, not of scabs. The 'snowdrops' are hated men who do odd jobs for the bureaucrats and are in their pockets. Donetzk is famous for its roses and there are said to be two rose-bushes for every member of the population – two million.

Perestroika in Donetzk!

The miners' battles

AS WE NEARED our destination, we saw the seedier side of housing conditions in Donetzk – soulless blocks of flats, dark courtyards and dingy stairways. But the welcome we received on arrival could not have been more grand. Lidia's mother is a typical *Babushka* – tonight a *Babushka* to the movement. She and Lidia have busied themselves in the kitchen to make sure a real feast is prepared. Not long after we had started the meal, a professional translator appeared. Yuri wanted to be sure that we got the most out of the evening.

We asked Yuri to give us material that we could publicise about the murder of Sotnikov, the Ukrainian miners' leader. 'This is not the first, nor the last, of attacks on members of the miners' Control Committees.' And Yuri proceeded to give us many examples, insisting we noted every name and every detail:

'At the Partizanskaya Mine in the city of Antratsit, the chair of the strike committee, AN Ostrapovitch, had been told by letter that he would be killed. At the Sixty Years of Soviet Ukraine mine, the director was deselected. Now, out of revenge, he is taking one of the miners to court for saying things that we know he didn't. He claims he was blackmailed. The court proceedings are continuing.

'SD Savuk, a member of the Strike Revision Committee at Slavyanoserbskya Mine, received constant threats over the phone. They were from a man calling himself a miner but who had never worked underground and had been told to go down by the workers' committee.

'At the Menshinskaya Mine in Pervomaisk, NA Solovya has also been threatened. He was the chairman of the Revision (Checking Committee, Workers' Control). He has been trying to stop the sales of alcohol out of hours – the only time it can be sold is between 2 and 7 pm.

'NN Kryzhanovski of the Alexandr Zapad Mine was severely beaten up by two miners from his own pit. He was personally responsible for checking the working of a shop. He found violations of their code of conduct and the shop assistant was dismissed. Her son and friends then beat him up.

'When the police investigated, they tried to make out it was non-political. They made him deny that his attackers had said that it was because he was a member of the strike control committee. He was concussed and confused, and his wife persuaded him to do this. She was worried that he would be beaten again unless he did. Now he is so frightened that he is asking for the two men to be released and the charges to be dropped.

'In Silidova, the first secretary of the City Party, the procurator of the city and other officials had a dacha built free of charge at the expense of the mine. The miners found out and made them pay. Just after this they made a provocation. A member of a co-operative came and offered money to the strikers – first 60 roubles, then 1000 roubles. When they took the money they were arrested. All the banknotes had been marked.

'The miners were put on remand. All the regional and republican papers reported that the strike committee had been taking bribes, extortion. The government was told that if these leaders were not released, there would be an all-out strike. They were released and the case was closed. No crime had been committed. However, only two papers reported the acquittal – unlike the publicity given to the "crime".'

Yuri's own deputy, who works at the Gorky mine, had been beaten up. His assailants said that it was because he was 'sticking his nose into other people's affairs'. So far no one has been found to be charged.

Leader murdered

More than a thousand miners had marched behind the coffin of Alexandrovich Sotnikov. Yuri told us he was a leading member of the co-ordinating council of the Donbas strike committees. He had received repeated letters with death threats as a result of his activities in exposing corruption at his mine – the 'Sixty Years of the Komsomol'. Nobody believed the official story that he was murdered in a drunken brawl after a party to celebrate the wedding of a neighbour. The autopsy showed that he died from pain shock which, the miners say, cannot happen when you're drunk – you don't feel pain!

Yuri said: 'It is known that those who were with him were drinking *Samagon* – home made vodka – but it is also known that those people did not kill him. We are sure that he was killed by the "snow-drops" – the *Podsnezhniki* – who take a salary as a miner but don't go underground.'

New management?

The discussion moved on to what had happened to the mine directors since the strike. We had read in the summer that, at Yuri's pit, the strikers had virtually taken over the running of the place. 'Well,' said Yuri, 'things have gone back a bit . . .

'The manager who was deposed at the time of the strike has now been reappointed. Seventy-eight per cent of the miners actually voted for him in the most recent election, which shows a different balance of forces. During the strike, 70 per cent had been against this man. Now, only 22 per cent are against him – but that manager pays high salaries. He also supported the 1 December strike – clever tactics.

'Besides, the voting was practically open – the curtains at the booths were hardly shut and there was only one name on the ballot form – so this is a victory for the system not for the man. After the election, he went to the hospital for a month and an engineer acted up as director. I personally asked the First Deputy Minister for Coal for a candidate to take his place. This Deputy Minister let me know that he would never do this because it violates the rules of the game. I had found some compromising material on this director and gave it to this First Deputy Minister but he would not take any notice of it.

'In my pit there is a hard core of a thousand miners who can act bravely. We managed to insist that the four most radical strikers should go to the university in Moscow on a course but the management sent a fifth man to spy on them while they were there.

'Management tried to sabotage our strike. They tried to switch off the electricity and allow the pits to fill with water and close. We were concerned to prevent explosions and any kind of damage. At first, the management didn't help us but then they closed ranks with us miners. At the Red Star Pit where the miners were not happy with the management, a completely new management was elected after the strike.'

The former secretary of the Party in Kolya's mine was pushed out after the strike (he says he retired!). 'He went to the pit and said that he was against strikes and that miners were the enemy of the people. The men shouted out "Are you going to refuse a new pension and the payment for night work that we won through our strike?"'

Kolya described himself as 'the grey cardinal of the strike committee'. He looked nothing like a cardinal and certainly did not have a grey personality.

'We're sick and tired of these "lighthouses" – the shock workers that you have seen in the photos, covered in medals. When Gorbachev came to Donetzk the miners with all these awards from the "period of stagnation" under Brezhnev were in the front line with their chests sticking out and they said that everything was OK down here. Since the strike we have no time for them.'

Stakhanov, Stalin's 'model miner' of the 1930's, was a local man. The myth about him reaching an individual record for coal production has been exploded. These miners confirmed it: 'All he did was the cutting. There was one person behind him picking up the coal, there were two propping up and others in turn providing them with timber. It was a whole team!'

Kolya had showed us gruesome photographs of two miners killed in the pit named after Stakhanov. We had heard of 10,000 deaths in the pits since 1980. He said the official figure was 8789 in the past nine years up to the 8 October – 489 this year. But they only count the deaths that actually occur underground and none of those that occur above ground, later in hospital, or elsewhere as a direct result of accidents.

Kolya told us about the wages and the conditions: 'Some miners get 320 roubles a month and wages depend on skill. The minimum is 200. The top grade is 7-800. That is for drivers and cutters. In some they can get as little as 350, even in the same mine. You can have one face which is good, where there is no collapse and you can reach the planned targets. In others which are wet, or where there are falls, it is impossible to reach the target. If you don't reach your planned targets, you don't get the money and you don't get paid for moving rock. The seams can be anything from 45 centimetres to 2 metres. At the Red Army Pit, it is hard work making the holes and shovelling the sand.'

'Revolutions themselves,' Sasha said, 'are not pleasant things – they mean bloodshed. We will try to achieve ours peacefully.'

End of an evening

Towards the end of twelve hours of discussion, these valiant strike leaders presented us with a calendar – 'In memory of our meeting – 4.11.89. Greetings of the Donetzk City Miners' Strike Committee'. Each wrote a message in the month of his or her birthday. Yuri's read: 'We shall live in a Europe without frontiers.'

Then the television news. In Vorkuta, a procurator had arrived and cancelled the order of the Regional Coal Board Director declaring their strike illegal! But the Don miners with us were angry at the lack of time given to the Vorkuta miners to put their own case.

The next item inflamed their tempers even more. A letter was read out on the TV purporting to come from the Donetzk Strike Committee, arguing against strike action because of the onset of winter. No such statement had been issued by the Donetzk Committee and our friends were adamant that, at the Strike Committee meeting the following day, they would smoke out the culprits.

As we watched the TV news together, anger gave way to delight at scenes of hundreds of thousands of defiant demonstrators in East Germany. Banners read: 'Socialism – Yes! Egonism – No!'. Then, for the first time on Soviet TV, Hungary 1956 was declared a popular uprising. 'Not long now for this country!' was the thought flooding through all our minds.

As we left, they gave us apples and flowers to take away with us. Babushka commented simply 'We understand each other without words'.

The Strike Committee meets

Entering the Strike Committee headquarters that Sunday morning, before the meeting was due to start, we were enthusiastically greeted by a Vorkuta miner. He was an envoy from the Strike Committee, travelling to mining areas and to Moscow to lobby the Supreme Soviet.

As the meeting started, the Vorkuta strike leader appealed for help. 'We have sent telegrams to every region. I haven't come to tell you to come out on strike with us, but simply to give you information about what is happening. Our strike is a complete strike, even though the press is saying otherwise.

'Our warning strike was declared illegal, and we were supposed to give back our wages. This angered us, and a majority of miners voted for further strike action.'

'Under what circumstances will you call off the strike?' asked one of the Don miners. 'When we have concrete proof of a date by which our demands will be granted.'

Another asked: 'Why has this not been sorted out by the government commission?' 'They refuse to come and talk to us.' Much discussion ensued about the Vorkuta strike, then a heated debate about whether additional political demands should be added to the miners' programme. Yuri intervened: 'This is 1989, not 1937 . . . If you go into a shop to buy bread, it is political.'

After that, an argument raged about where the statement read out on television had come from. The Committee leaders were convinced that the Party had had a hand in it. Both the local Party boss and the police chief were present at this meeting! The issue remained unresolved, and further verbal battles took place over the programme of demands, complaints about conditions in the pits and even a suggestion that the Committee should be disbanded.

It was proposed that collections be taken to support the Vorkuta miners and that someone be sent to visit them. It was also agreed that measures be taken to recover the money donated by every miner in the USSR during the British miners' strike. They had all given a day's pay out of international solidarity, but had been told by their government that Thatcher had refused to let the money reach the British miners. Now they wanted to know, if it had not reached the British miners, where was it? Perhaps they could have it back to pursue their own dispute.

In the smoking break, a long resolution was drawn up by Yuri. The night before, he was supposed to have been on a late programme, but had been excluded. The Strike Committee were going to demand time to put their case on television. Now, he was insisting 'The case must be in a language that everyone can understand and as near to 9 pm (prime viewing time) as possible.' There followed more disputes, one walk out and a number of decisions!

Before the meeting finally broke up, we were given the chance to convey greetings from the British Labour movement. As socialists and 'friends of workers' MP Terry Fields', we promised to organise support in Britain and internationally – for the Vorkuta miners and for the struggle for workers' democracy and socialism everywhere. We offered a donation to the Donetzk Strike Committee and gained the warmest response when we undertook on their behalf to find out what had happened to the money they donated for the British miners.

As the meeting concluded, we were once again gently mobbed. Everyone wanted our names and addresses and we had the impression that they would have stayed with us for another two or three hours talking and exchanging views about what was happening in the world.

At the back of the platform in the hall hung a portrait of Lenin, and a slogan of his declaring: 'Coal is the real bread of industry!' This reminded us that nobody had eaten or drunk anything for hours. We were destined to go another 16 hours before we had a meal – a light breakfast.

A visit to the pit

Then we go with Alexandr to visit his pit, the Zashyadko. It is the eve of the holiday break, so the place is nearly deserted. We see a few workers being interviewed by the administration before they start their shift. The managers, some in wide, peasant-type caps, look quite ordinary, quite proletarian. It is strange to hear the word 'comrade' being used universally – we hear it in offices, buses, shops, anywhere when people communicate.

In Alexandr's 'union office', he explains that the old union would be very difficult to reform. 'It is an organisation that has been in charge for 70 years. The miners are sick of hearing that the trade unions are a "school of communism". In March, there was an official conference of the miners' union at which demands for new elections to the STKs and the union committees were forcefully put.

'In this pit there are 5,400 miners, 10,000 workers altogether. Along with the pit itself goes a state farm, a palace of culture, house-building, administration of the hostels etc. We have our own representatives on the STK. I am on the STK and on the Strike Committee, too.'

Although Alexandr is a Russian, he is a member of *Rukh*, the Ukrainian Popular Front that is supposedly nationalistic. 'It was set up,' he says, 'to fight for *Perestroika* and unite all democratic organisations. The word literally means "movement" – it is the "Popular Ukrainian Movement for *Perestroika*".'

The Ukraine is the most important industrial republic in the USSR with a 50 million population. 'Only a tiny part of *Rukh*'s programme is anti-Russian,' Alexandr assures us. 'This area had bitter experiences of Stalinism. Thirty thousand were shot in this town in 1937.'

'Many of the miners come from outside Donetzk and need accommodation but at present there are 12,000 on the waiting list. Some of them are living in the hostels – four to a room in some cases. Even families have to live in one room.'

'Faces in this pit are around 1.6 metres high. One or two of them are 36 or 40 degrees of heat, when they should be around 24. The average of fatalities here in a year is three.'

We came out of the office complex and made our way towards the pit head. Once more, brass band music blared out over loudspeakers into the cold night air. No one was about. It was all eerie *1984*-ish experience.

We took the path to the badly-lit, badly-ventilated, stuffy building that housed the pit-shaft. A few miners were sitting on a bench with

116

their helmets and their boiler-suits on, waiting to go down. A loud clanking noise signalled the approach of something dangerous. As it got even louder, a massive metal hopper on wheels trundled into view and onto the platform of one of the cages. A woman in a rough, padded jacket carried out the necessary operations just to put it safely into the mine. This did not look like light work by any means!

A TV programme that night about Lenin examined in the minutest detail where he stood on numerous famous occasions, who stood beside him, what the place was like now etc. There was archive film and photographs including impressive shots of demonstrations on Marsovo Pole – the Mars Field – in Leningrad. The extent to which Lenin has been 'deified' is horrifying. He would be turning in his mausoleum!

In spite of the turning-away from Lenin and his ideas because of the crimes committed in his name, there are many in this society who still look to him for inspiration. The programme and ideas of both Lenin and Trotsky are eagerly studied by those looking for a way out on the basis of the socialist planned economy. Foremost amongst these will be many miners.

Return to Leningrad

THE NEXT DAY, we were on our way to Leningrad. It is beautiful from the air. We feel as if we are really 'coming home'! But unpleasant things can happen here, too.

That evening, in the Bulgarian restaurant, two women are unceremoniously moved to our table from another one before they have finished their meal. A malicious-looking woman has just passed money to a waiter, looking him in the eye as much as to say 'Make sure we get a table to ourselves or things will happen to you'. She, and her equally unpleasant partner, sit down at the now-vacant table for four, unmolested by workers on a night out to celebrate the revolution! 'The *mafia*!' is the women's simple explanation to us.

Anniversary protest

November 7th dawns – the 72nd Anniversary of the October Revolution. Opera music blares out over loud-hailers in the town – enough to put you off it for life! A human flood moves toward the centre of the city with balloons, flags, children. The whole population seems to be on the move.

The official demonstration will end up in Winter Palace Square. We make our way to join the unofficial organisations, who have planned to have their own 'feeder' march for the first time since the days of the Left Opposition. Twelve to fifteen thousand have turned out. Last spring, there was a rally of 60,000 in the Kirov stadium but they say there has never been a street demonstration this big.

The delight on the faces of the organisers is indescribable. They see it as the breaking of a log jam, opening the way for bigger and bigger and more and more assertive demonstrations from now on. Bright banners wave as the march speeds past factories with tall chimneys.

At the Fontanka Canal, the unofficial demonstration is stopped.

118

Will it be allowed to join with the official demonstration or is there going to be trouble? A nervous but excited mood affects the whole gathering. The official demonstration passes over the bridge and down the other side of the canal. Some balloons float on the water. The 'unofficials' begin to jeer and whistle at the 'officials'. The 'officials' are silent. Then they begin to wave – hostility dissolves. There are cheers on either side.

The end of the official contingent crosses the bridge. The 'oppositionists' link arms to protect their demonstration in case the authorities now decide to make an attack.

No one can believe it is happening when they are allowed peacefully to join on at the end of the main demonstration. They move freely and happily beside the canal and towards Dzerzhinsky Street. Here the loudspeakers on the buildings relay news of the official demonstration and also of the unofficial demonstration. Cheers go up. The euphoria is infectious. You feel as if everything has been gained when it is just the first step!

People we have met before tell us there are police participating on the demonstration out of uniform. One of our Narodny Front friends makes an appeal to a band on the pavement who are just packing up their instruments. They have been with the official demonstration. They are a little tired and reluctant to join another march, but 'We are with you', they declare.

Winter Palace Square

Buses block the side streets. The tension mounts as we near the Winter Palace Square itself. Will our path be blocked? Unbelievably, our column proceeds, slowly but surely, into the centre of the square. Party bureaucrats and military top brass stand like wooden figures on the podium, repeating old slogans, looking for some response. The 'hurrahs' they hear are not for their slogans but for those of the protesters! 'Power to the people – Hurrah!' 'Down with the Partocracy!' 'Hurrah!'

Fists and victory-V signs are shaken at these humiliated 'dummies'. Then we look back and see that Komsomolist 'goons' in track-suits and holding tall banners like pikes have moved in and blocked the path of the 'unofficials'. One part of the demonstration is now separated from the other. It looks as if perhaps trouble could be in store. But, no . . . The other half of the demonstration comes round to the front, so that the whole square is now full of oppositionists.

There are all sorts of political tendencies represented. There are one or two black flags; there are many red. Democratic Union supporters complain that there is too much red on this demonstration and not enough white.

There are placards that read 'Power to the Soviets, not the Party', 'Let's Build Socialism!', 'Medicine for all, not the chosen few!'. 'Take the palaces off the bureaucrats, return them to the theatres and the cinemas!' All layers are here, putting forward demands on the issues that affect them most.

What a contrast to the lifeless slogans of the official demonstration! 'Glory to 72' (Years of the revolution), 'Fulfil the decisions of the 27th Congress'. 'Produce items on time of good quality'.

One group of burly oppositionists yells 'Down with Marxism!' But what can you expect? The bureaucracy has carried out all of its crimes in the name of Marxism. Once the protests start, everything associated with them is rejected and howled down.

What next?

The exhilarated crowd, having taken the square, has achieved a mighty first blow against the bureaucracy – beyond their wildest dreams. They could hardly believe it themselves. They stood for a few minutes in wonder and amazement, drinking in the situation. Soldiers, sailors, police in the Square are bewildered too – uneasy, but, in some cases, visibly delighted about what is happening. There is no violence.

Then the 'unofficials' move off quietly, separating to go over the canal bridges, and coming together as one vast sea to cross the Neva by the great Kirov Bridge, and to assemble on the other side for an open-air meeting.

At the Lenin Theatre, a jubilant crowd is addressed from the steps. The popular deputy, Ivanov, surrounded by colourful placards and banners, takes the loud-hailer. He is not a fiery speaker but you get the impression, without even hearing one word of his programme, that most of his audience would go to the end of the earth for him. They simply know his record as an outspoken opponent of the regime; that is sufficient for the moment.

Vasili is here at the demonstration with friends from his union. They have a banner, a simple banner, which reads 'We support the striking miners'. Vasili has met some representatives of Polish *Solidarity* and is over the moon, but he points at us and says, 'but they don't like *Solidarity*!' He is so happy participating in this demonstration after 20 years of boycotting the official procession, that he prefers not to differ with us over anything.

'We support the striking miners'

Ivanov speaks at the Lenin Theatre

Leaflets and journals are once again snatched up and a warm response is given to every speaker. The crowd has grown by the minute and seems reluctant to leave the park once the official 'unofficial' proceedings are over. People stay around to listen to the more eccentric speakers – a dissident 'poet', a Democratic Union extremist and others who take the mike. Such is the magnanimity of the movement at the present undiscriminating stage, everyone feels that, if you are lucky enough to be able to hold a meeting without it being broken up, you should allow anyone a chance to speak. If you produce a paper, it should be a platform for various opinions. Differentiation will no doubt take place at a later, more serious and critical stage.

That evening we discuss with some of our old acquaintances. They express enthusiastic interest in what we have seen in Moscow and above all in Donetzk. The strike in Vorkuta continues, and the miners there are seen as the standard-bearers for the whole movement against the Partocracy.

At precisely nine o'clock in the evening, fireworks are let off throughout the city to celebrate the victory of October. At every bang and explosion, children cheer from the bridges, giggling with delight. If only the mountains of hypocrisy could be removed, these celebrations would be the highlight of the socialist calendar.

The quest for clarity

On one of our last evenings, we met some people tending in the direction of social democracy who want to set up a new party. 'Without a programme,' they began, 'any organisation will remain a small organisation. But the only ones who have a worked out programme are those that want to go back to Stalinist dictatorship and those who want capitalism!'

'People don't believe in the powers-that-be party anymore. But you can't just take hold of the Swedish model, or the German model, or the pre-1917 model, or private ownership. We haven't had and we won't have private ownership on a large scale.

'Russians look at things differently from people in the West. Their approach stems from harsh conditions, the crushing of individuality etc. Some workers are so brutalised they work only grudgingly, some workers work out of solidarity. Shop-workers are happier if they have no customers.

'We are aiming for a new party, but we think there will be several and we don't want a situation where people are saying "We're the real Social Democrats and you're not". There is going to be a social democratic conference in Tallinn in January and there will be "liberal" and "labour" wings. In Leningrad, we are closer to the labour position. One hundred and eighty delegates are expected plus 30 observers, 50 guests and 40 press.'

We struggled to get them to explain exactly what they are in favour of. 'Are you *for* privatisation?' 'Maybe, we are not sure.' 'Are you *for* the market?' 'Probably, but that is a difficult question.' Everything was 'difficult'!

These two activists were intensely interested in change and obviously very busy producing journals, organising conferences, etc. One of them, Anatoly, had read quite extensively, including the works of Trotsky, but when it came to the way ahead and a clear programme, they were totally uncertain.

Eventually we outlined the simple programme of Lenin with the modern additions. 'Is that clear?' 'Mmm! Yes! Very clear!' We had no illusions that, because of this answer, these particular people would henceforth be convinced Trotskyists. Far from it. But the fact that even these 'erudite' political debaters could find nothing with which to counter our arguments encouraged us.

Before this discussion, waiting at the Metro station, we saw the biggest queue of all. People were intent on getting something 'top secret'. It was so secret, nobody would tell us anything. We thought perhaps that there was still some 'unofficial' revolutionary newspaper we had not yet been able to get our hands on.

When the people we were meeting joined us, we asked them what this was all for. They laughed and told us it was spy stories under the title 'Top Secret!' Well, life has been so full of surprises, we wouldn't be surprised if we were surprised again!

Last evening

Vasili's eyes are dancing with delight – the Berlin Wall has come down! 'But Krenz said only last week "The wall will stand for another hundred years". Thousands have gone across into West Berlin, had a look and come back.'

Together, we discuss the importance of internationalism, the role of a workers' paper and especially the perspectives for the coming years, touching again on the National Question – now a central issue.

Already, powerful centrifugal and reactionary tendencies are showing themselves. In the absence of a clear leadership to the workers' movements, further bloodbaths could be in store. We could see the beginnings of a break up of society and even of a return to barbarism. The threat of chaos could provide the pretext for the use of the iron fist – either by Gorbachev himself to avoid being ousted from power, or by the hard-liners to force a return to centralisation and Stalinist methods. Bare shelves, refugees, housing crises, land hunger and even a struggle for control over local resources have fuelled and exacerbated the national question.

No solution to the national question will be found on the basis of bureaucratic rule, we agree. This is still responsible for wide-spread violations of many basic civil rights and fundamental principles of socialism.

The serious talking on these matters gave way to celebration of our visit – a little eating and drinking and one more exchange of jokes.

Brezhnev looks at a statue of Chekhov: 'Who's that?' 'That's Chekhov, comrade Leonid Ilyich!' 'Oh, yes, I know, he wrote *Mumu* (child's book to be found in everyone's home), didn't he?' 'I'm sorry comrade Leonid Ilyich, but that was Turgenev!' 'That's strange, they've put up a statue to the wrong man!'

And ours for them: 'You know there was a terrible fire at the home of US vice-president Dan Quayle. It totally destroyed the whole of his library! It was a tragedy, all three books were burnt to a cinder and one of them he hadn't even finished colouring in!'

With the world's leaders, past and present, suitably put down, we left our friends and, the following morning, left Leningrad and the Soviet Union.

Awaiting us on the plane were numerous free copies of the *Moscow News* with a special assessment of Trotsky's role along with Lenin at the head of the Russian Revolution.

Postscript

In the space of a few weeks between the first manuscript of this book being prepared and going to print, events in the USSR have unfolded with lightning speed. Mass pressure from below is forcing the abolition of Article Six. Street demonstrations and strike struggles have removed Party leaderships in towns, cities and regions across the Soviet Union – from Volgograd in the Ukraine to Tyumen in Siberia – the biggest oil and gas-producing area in the world.

In the local elections, the ruling party has suffered ignominious defeats. Lithuania has broken from the centre and powerful pro-independence, even nationalist, movements have developed in nearly every republic. The biggest opposition demonstrations since the October Revolution have been seen in Moscow and other cities.

Gorbachev is accruing to himself greater personal powers than even Thatcher or General de Gaulle, in an attempt to ride out the coming storms.

History is gathering pace. Waves of revolution and ebbs of counter-revolution will succeed each other in rapid succession. For the workers of Eastern Europe and the USSR, there is no longer any point in looking to the East – to China where political dinosaurs maintain their iron grip. 'There must be some other way', these workers say as they look to the West. They hope against hope that someone, somewhere, has a solution.

Events in Sweden and elsewhere have confirmed that there is no safe haven or secure future for capitalism. The attempts of a Social Democratic government to impose cuts in real wages have been met with ferocious resistance on the part of the Swedish working class. Daily, our analysis and approach is being borne out in the course of a perpetual struggle – now beneath the surface, now open – of living class forces.

All the objective elements that make for a new October exist in the Soviet Union – only there is no Marxist Party. All the classical conditions for a successful revolution against the old order are maturing.

The ruling layer is split and uncertain of how to proceed, whether through concession or repression. They are afflicted with a profound feeling that they are a doomed force in society. The middle layers are deserting them and expressing all their dissatisfactions in the ferment of debate, discussion and protest. The proletariat has flexed its muscles, and giant strike movements have welled up from below. No longer cowed by the threat of fascism or war, after generations of being deprived of control and management of society, they have begun to impose their will.

Everyone knows what they are against, but only a conscious leadership like that of the Bolsheviks in 1917 can harness the energies of the masses and lead to the successful transformation of society. The creation of such a party has been put firmly on the agenda. The gathering of the necessary forces will be no easy task, but the raw material is already to hand. The impressions of our visit have been confirmed by much recent material in the British press and on television, that the working people of the Soviet Union have lost not only their fear, but their indifference. They display a burning desire, not only to speak their minds, but to challenge the rule of the bureaucracy. If the call is given, they will be prepared to enter into a struggle to change society.

Once the proletariat of Leningrad and Moscow, and the miners of Siberia and the Ukraine, move in their millions into decisive battles, the momentous events of 1989 will be dwarfed. National rivalries and hatreds will be burnt out in the course of these mighty social movements. Lasting victory can only be assured if Marxists with a clear understanding, strategy and programme can come to the head of the movement.

In the situation which now unfolds, the ideas of scientific socialism can gain support rapidly. So too, in the absence of a clear alternative, unfortunately, can ill-founded illusions in capitalism. The opposition 'democratic' movement runs the risk of being derailed by such alien ideas.

Our visit has revealed that the political consciousness of the mighty proletariat of the Soviet Union has undoubtedly been thrown back as a result of the decades of Stalinism, but it can be rapidly restored in the white heat of the coming events. Recession in the West will shatter many a dream. But nothing, especially a revolution, is an automatic process!

Marxism as a theory, method and set of ideas, will be as invaluable a weapon to the fighters of the present generation as they were to the Bolsheviks who led the successful socialist revolution of 1917. Those who have trampled in the mud the ideals of October, the red banner of the world proletariat and the humble aspirations of

125

the toiling masses of all countries, have more than enough to answer for. Their crimes must be avenged!

A clear rallying call for workers' democracy must be sounded without delay. Once more the course of human history could hang on the outcome of great events in the USSR. The victorious political revolution here and in Eastern Europe will lay the basis at last for the creation of a new world.

Elizabeth Clarke and Richard Peters

March 1990

Translation of letter sent by Labour MPs Terry Fields (Liverpool Broadgreen), Dave Nellist (Coventry SE) and Pat Wall (Bradford N) to striking miners.

Dear Comrades,

We read about your meeting of unofficial trade union groups with great interest.

We are Socialist (Labour) members of the English Parliament, representing the towns of Liverpool, Coventry and Bradford. As workers' representatives, we consider ourselves bound to live on workers' wages under the slogan 'A Workers' MP on a Worker's Wage'. That is, we accept not the huge salary of a bourgeois MP, but only the average wage of those we represent. The surplus we return to the labour movement. Our accounts are presented to the labour movement for scrutiny.

As Socialists and Internationalists, we therefore send you our greetings and support to your group and we would like to hear your experiences and aspirations from you. We would like to offer you any help possible.

We are campaigning for a socialist solution to the difficulties faced by workers under capitalism, such as, for example, unemployment, poor living conditions and lowering of wages. Such a solution demands, not only such reforms as a reduction in the working week and a national living wage, but also a planned economy under workers' control and management.

Like you, we want to ensure that such a society will be free from bureaucratism and corruption, and will be organised by and in the interests of, the worker. We therefore fully agree with the conditions laid down by Lenin for the establishment of a democratic workers' state.

1   Not only the election, but the right of recall at any time.
2   Wages no higher than the wages of the workers.
3   Immediate transition to the position where, for a time, all become bureaucrats and therefore, no-one becomes a bureaucrat.
4   No standing army but the armed people.

It seems to us that, in the light of historical experience, workers need the following democratic rights. A planned economy needs democracy like the body needs oxygen. Therefore, we support the following demands:

*   Free trade unions independent of the state
*   Freedom of speech, the press and assembly
*   The right of free elections with the participation of all political parties except the fascists. We believe that the only way to prevent bureaucratism and corruption is the control of the economy by the workers and not simply in their name. Independent trade unions are very important. As Lenin said, they are necessary 'to defend the workers from their state and also to get them to protect our state'.

Despite the economic boom over the last few years, terrible difficulties face workers today in capitalist society. Even the capitalists themselves expect a crisis in two or three years. And it is true that a mass movement will develop against capitalism in the West.

Our campaign for an international democratic socialist society would be much stronger if we were able to exchange our experiences with comrades who are waging a similar campaign in the USSR.

We intend to raise this matter in Parliament and hope that it is possible we meet with you so as to further discuss our views.

We await your reply with great interest.

Terry Fields, Dave Nellist, Pat Wall.

Appendix Two

Excerpts from the programme of the Trade Union *Justice*

Join our independent Trade Union. It will defend your interests, it will defend your rights and freedoms.

Our trade union will fight **against** arbitrary rule and lawlessness, against the abuse of the feelings and dignity of the common person, subordination by the administration and against the complete independence of the directors of enterprises.

Our trade union will fight **for** an increase in the share of the income of an enterprise in wages; for an increase in the wages of those who labour – those who create the value.

Our trade union will fight **for** improved living standards, for the abolition of manual labour and heavy work, especially for women, for an increase in the productivity of labour – not by intensification and production lines, but by improving working conditions, by the lightening of work, the reduction in the strain of work by mechanisation and automation.

Our trade union will fight so that all the means created by the workers are invested to improve working lives, the way of life of the workers.

The prosperity of the country – this does not only mean the prosperity of the bureaucrats and directors of the state, but is most of all the prosperity of the majority of workers.

Join our Trade Union in order to fight, to fight together for our interests, for our freedom and our prosperity.

Points from the Programme:

*   Payments for periods of disability independent of official Trade Union membership; we demand an urgent solution to this injustice to millions of workers.

* For an increase in wages as a proportion of national income or profit of the enterprise to a minimum of 50 per cent.
* Introduction of pay rises linked to rising prices, calculated by the Index of Living Standards.
* Abolition of piece work rates – introduction of a high hourly rate.
* Abolition of the unjust differential between administrators and workers and between workers themselves.
* An increase in the enterprises' income due to increased production should lead to a growth in real wages. Pay rates should be simple and understandable to every worker, even as far as the principles of the allocation of the whole income/balanace of the factory is concerned.
* The appraisal and promotion of workers should not depend on his participation in the 'social life' or 'social status' as it is now; nor in the same way on his Party membership or as a political stalwart.

Re: the Distribution of the Leningrad Budget:

* Stop unnecessary overheads for the workers, on capital and other buildings in Leningrad.
* Increase the expenditure on culture, education, training and public health.

The Abolition of the Barracks Position:

* The abolition of the unified command and hegemony of the directors and foremen. Their full election on a competitive basis – without approval from above and without (the threat of) the disqualification from training or social benefits.
* The right to take jobs, change jobs or resign without control.
* Abolition of all internal passports.
* Abolition of hostel regulations, the election of their hostel 'commandants' by the work collectives, their submission to the hostel's council.
* The creation of a just state – the right to free speech, the press, the right to receive and disseminate information, the right guaranteed by law to use the press, typography, radio and television. Television to be under the control of a public

committee. Full independence of factory newspapers from the plant administration.
* Freedom of Trade Unions, workers' associations independent of the state and the Party.

Social Guarantees:

* 40 hour working week. Abolition of 'black' Saturdays.
* Minimum pension of 70% of wages – abolition of all personal pensions.
* Alteration of the income tax, indirect and sales taxes in the interests of the workers.
* Introduction of an inheritance tax.

Declaration of the Leningrad Trade Union *Independence*:

Workers!

The position of the working class is worsening. The intensification of physical labour is rising. The administration does not pay extra in working wages. The outlay of physical strength is more than our wages. The inability of the leaders to organise production overstrains the muscles of the workers. There is an increase in traumatisation, intensification of fatal accidents. Tiredness and the deterioration of the workers' strength are reaching their limits.

The conflict between the workers and the administration is sharpening. The strike movement is growing. Workers who defend their professional interests are dismissed on any pretext. The working person has no rights in industry or in society. In the courts, appeals are useless – the laws are anti-worker. The Soviet of Workers' Collectives has been transformed into the obedient instrument of the plant director. The State trade unions are not in a position to defend the interests of the workers. So to live and work is increasingly impossible. The time is approaching to unite the workers in the struggle to strengthen their position.

A professional association of workers – *Independence*

For a united fight for the professional rights and freedoms has been created in Leningrad. It has a non-bureaucratic, self-ruling structure. The trade union *Independence* is organised by the Initiative Committee for the Association of Workers, the members of which represent workers of different plants.

Workers! Unite in any groups of two or more people according to profession, present your demands to the foreman, chief of the section or director of the plant. Workers in such united groups automatically become members of the trade union *Independence*.

Workers! United, you receive the right to present professional class demands directly to the administration in the name of the trade union *Independence*, by-passing the bureaucratic dispute commissions, trade union committees and work councils.

Workers, delegate your leaders from the united occupational groups to the committees of workers' self-management for the sections and plants for the organisation of workers' assemblies, mass meetings, demonstrations and strikes.

Workers! Unite, join the struggle against arbitrary administration, sharply formulate your demands, persistently strive for their implementation, form your strike fund. Do so and you have your trade union *Independence*.

A headquarters has been formed for the co-ordination of the general activities of the trade union *Independence* and it will consult with all interested parties on your questions.

Declaration of the Regional Union of Strike Committees of the Donbas

A. General position, aims, tasks and rights.

1.   The Regional Union of Miners' Strike Committees of the Donbas is a social organisation uniting on voluntary principles the strike committees of the towns, industrial units, mines, enterprises and organisation of the coal industry of the Donbas.

   The activity of the Union is to build on the basis of self-management, openness and solidarity in the achievement of general aims. The Union acts in accordance with the constitution of the USSR, the Declaration of Human Rights and with Soviet law. The co-ordinating council of the Union and its executive committee serves as the authorised representation entered into by the Union of miners' strike committees of the Donbas.

2.   The main aim of the Union is the furtherance of *Perestroika*, the democratic transformation of society, the movement towards a just state, the development of a civilian and just authority, the real defence of the legal rights and the interests of the workers in the coal industry and their families.

3.   The basic task of the Union is control over the implementation of the demands of the miners in accordance with the minutes of the measures agreed between the miners' strike committees of the towns of the Donbas and the Commission of the Council of Ministers of the USSR signed in the course of the July Donbas miners' strike.

   The tasks of the Union are also:

3.1.   To render assistance to the work collectives in the solution of conflicts and dispute situations.

3.2.   To take decisions on the calling of strikes, returning to work, and the suspension or discontinuing of strikes including warning, partial and general strikes, bound with the strike authority of the pits enterprises and organisations serving as members of the Union.

3.3.   To study, generalise, disseminate and introduce the most important experiences of industrial self-management.

3.4.   To organise and consolidate the bonds of the work collectives with one another, the establishment and implementation of contact 43 with workers' organisations of other countries.

3.5.   To manifest workers' solidarity.

4.   The Union will collaborate with state, social and other organisations and enterprises and individual citizens in the work of *Perestroika* in reorganising economic mechanisms and the expansion of independent workers' collectives.

5.   In accordance with its tasks the Union will:

5.1.   Conduct meetings, conferences, demonstrations, discussions, lectures, referenda.

5.2.   Realise the preparation of information materials, projects, proposals for action in appropriate state, social and other organisations and even in the organs of the means of mass information.

5.3.   Publish its material through all the means of mass information of the region, including the TV and radio of Donetsk, Dnepropetrovsk, Voroshilovgradsk, Rostovsk *oblasts* and even the *oblast*, town, regional newspapers and newspapers of the enterprises and organisations in the name of *oblast* in the course of 24 hours from the moment of presentation to the editor and even to have our own means of mass information.

6.   Decisions of the Union, taken within the bounds of its authority, are binding on the administrations of the members of the work collectives of the enterprises joined to the Union.

B. Members of the Union – their rights and responsibilities.

1.   Membership of the Union is open to town strike committees, manufacturing Unions, miners, enterprises and organisations of the coal industry of the Donbas.

The strike committees who join the Union can have their own rules.

2.   Strike Committees in the Union have the right:

2.1.   To use the organisation, information channels and other help of the Union for the resolution of problems arising from their activities, resulting from their constitutional tasks.

2.2.   To choose delegates to the conferences of the Union, to participate in the formation of the leading bodies of the Union.

2.3.   To consider the question of the work of the Union and to implement the resolutions to improve its work.

2.4.   To receive information from the state, social, co-operative and other enterprises, Unions, organisations and establishments, including access to documents of their financial economic activities.

2.5.   To place before their own bodies questions about the responsibilities of functionaries, encroaching on the rights of the work collectives and individual citizens.

2.6.   Members of strike committees who are part of the Union have the statu of immunity in agreement with Paragraph 19 of the 'Protocol'.

2.7.   Members of the town and combined strike committee, who are part of the Union, are freed from basic work with the retention of average wages and all the privileges according to their place of work.

3.   Strike committees who are part of the Union are bound:

3.1.   To observe the rules of the Union.

3.2.   To participate in the implementation of its tasks.

3.3.   To participate in the creation of the Union's funds.

3.4.   Members of the Union, in breach of the rules can be excluded from the Union by decision of the conference.

Amidst all the material on the Soviet Union and Eastern Europe currently available, a few stand out, either as indispensible to an understanding of events, or as providing the only clear Marxist analysis of Stalinism and its methods. The following are a few of those we would recommend:

History of the Russian Revolution .... Trotsky
Revolution Betrayed .... Trotsky
Ten Days that Shook the World.. Reed
On Kronstadt .... Trotsky and Lenin
In the name of the working class.. Kopacsi
The Other Europe .... Rupnik

Pamphlets:

Ideals of October.. LPYS
Russia — reform or revolution .... Grant
Russia — how the bureaucracy seized power .... Collins
Eyewitness in China .... Jolly
Stalinism in Crisis... Grant and Taaffe

All of the above books can be obtained by writing to:
World Socialist Books, 3/13 Hepscott Road, London E9 5HB.

Special Offers from FORTRESS BOOKS

The Unbroken Thread
The Development of Trotskyism over 40 years—Selected writings of Ted Grant

608 pages, many photos
Special offer, the Hardback (cover price £11.95) for the softback price £6.95. 5 copies for £30
An invaluable collection of Marxist writings covering 1938-83, charting the development of Marxist ideas through the 1939-45 war, the rise of Stalinism in Eastern Europe, the post war boom, the colonial revolution and the crisis of British capitalism.

Month of Revolution
by Clare Doyle

80 pages, £1.95 (cover price £2.50). 5 copies for £8
A vivid account of the tumultuous events in France 1968.

Liverpool—A City That Dared to Fight
by Peter Taaffe and Tony Mulhearn

528 pages. Hardback £9.95 (cover price £14.95)
Softback £6.95, 5 copies for £25
'A fascinating self-portrait...told with imagery redolent of Petrograd 1917.' The Independent 25/1/88

Out of the Night
by Jan Valtin

712 pages, hardback only £7.95 (cover price £9.95), 5 copies for £35
A classic socialist autobiography, outlining the life and struggles of a Communist Party trade union activist in Germany 1918-38.

Germany—From Revolution to Counter Revolution
by Rob Sewell

96 pages, £2 (cover price £2.50). 5 copies for £8.50
Covers events in Germany from the 1918 revolution to the rise of Hitler in 1933, drawing out the lessons for the movement today.

Order from World Socialist Books, or direct from Fortress Books, PO Box 141 London E2 ORL. Postage—please add 20% on orders under £5, 10% on orders £5-£10. Over £10 post free.